557
SCH   Schuberth, Christopher J.

A view of the past: an
introduction to Illinois
geology

A View of the Past

Frontispiece. Interlocking, cube-shaped crystals of fluorite, the State Mineral of Illinois. Usually purple or lavender, fluorite also occurs in delicate shades of honey and amber. (Illinois State Museum Collection)

A VIEW OF THE PAST

An Introduction to Illinois Geology

by
Christopher J. Schuberth
Associate Curator of Education

Published by the
ILLINOIS STATE MUSEUM

Illinois State Museum
Springfield, Illinois
1986

1986
ISSN 0360-0297
ISBN 0-89792-104-6
(Printed by Authority of the State of Illinois)
(54352—4M—7-86)

Time is the way Mother Nature has of preventing
everything from happening at once.

— from an old wit whose name time has erased.

Contents

List of Figures

List of Tables

Preface

Imagine the State of Illinois as it appeared in the beginning of the immense span of time before life developed here. Upon the land there were no trees, no leafy oaks, no elms, no maples, nor even representatives of the ancient conifers. There was no growth upon the prairies—no red-hued prairie grass, no waving cornfield, no rippling wheat. There were no houses, no cities, farms or people. For the geological story of Illinois begins with the very young world of long, long ago, before most of the landscape features were shaped or sculptured in their present form.

So began the booklet in the Illinois State Museum's Story of Illinois Series, *The Past Speaks to You,* authored by Ann Livesay. Published in 1951 and reprinted in 1965, this booklet was no longer available after 1975. New developments in understanding the geology of Illinois dictated that a publication be prepared incorporating these new ideas. *A View of the Past: An Introduction to Illinois Geology* is that publication. As such, it will not help to identify rock, mineral, or fossil specimens found in the Illinois countryside; other publications are available for that purpose. It will, however, tell how the better-known minerals or fossils or rocks got where they are and how each fits into the broad geologic character of the region. More importantly, this publication will relate all the physical events that affected Illinois from time immemorial, from more than 1.5 billion years ago until the present. It will do this in chronologic order, describing not the human history of the state but the geologic history of a land before people arrived in the Midwest, a land that slowly evolved to become that familiar place now known as Illinois.

Facing page. Cave-In-Rock, 20 feet high and 30 feet wide, is dissolved into 300-million-year-old limestone at Cave-In-Rock State Park, Hardin County, along the Ohio River.

Many persons assisted me in this project. I am especially grateful to Drs. James E. King, Russell W. Graham, Jeffrey J. Saunders, and Richard L. Leary, all research curators in the geological sciences at the Illinois State Museum. Their critical readings of the manuscript, discussions, and suggestions were most helpful. Dr. Leon Follmer and David Reinertsen, both of the Illinois State Geological Survey, as well as many of their colleagues, added measurably in improving the accuracy of the text; they patiently assisted, also, in identifying and acquiring many of the needed photographs from their files. Any errors or ambiguities that remain in the text are solely my responsibility. Gary Ori, photographer for the Illinois Office of Education, provided the full-color frontispiece of the fluorite specimen, the official mineral of Illinois. All other photographs, unless otherwise noted, are by the author.

Finally, but not least, I am indebted to many other staff members of the Illinois State Museum: Marlin Roos, who converted many of my color slides into black-and-white prints and photographed the rock, mineral, and fossil specimens; Nancy Wells for editing, proofreading, and designing this publication; Julianne Snider for designing the cover and preparing some of the maps and other illustrations; Betsy Newman for deciphering and converting my long-hand heiroglyphics into readable, typed pages; and to Karen Pierceall and Nancy Lohrasbi for entering the entire manuscript on the word processor. To all, I am most grateful.

Chapter 1
Introduction

Coal—fluorite—petroleum—limestone—sand and gravel—tripoli—galena: What have all these seemingly unrelated materials in common? All are rock and mineral resources found in Illinois, and all are of significant economic value to the state today (Fig. 1-1). All, too, were products of the past—the far, distant geologic past. So, also, were the sea-dwelling trilobites and ammonites, the elephantlike mastodons and mammoths, and the giant seed ferns. None of these live today; they are vestiges of the past. A familiarity with rocks and minerals, an understanding of how they came to be, and knowledge of the circumstances that brought about the extinction of once-living plants and animals known from the fossil record are some of the many items that are of interest to the geologist.

But geology is more than a curiosity about minerals, rocks, and fossils. It is the study of the whole Earth, not only its materials and its internal structure—how the minerals and rocks are arranged and distributed underground—but also the study of its mountains, plateaus, and plains and how they came to be; its oceans, rivers, and lakes; of erosion here and sediment deposition there; the why and wherefore of volcanic eruptions and the sudden and often catastrophic shifting of the ground by earthquakes. Geology is the study of all that is physical about the Earth; the processes at work on the surface and below; how the continents and oceans have changed through time; and why petroleum or lead formed in some places and not in others. It is the study of the kinds of ancient plants and animals that once lived and flourished on the lands of the Earth and in its seas and the ancient environments in which they lived. Many of these creatures, and

Facing page. Drilling for crude oil in Clay County. Oil production in Illinois averaged 79,000 barrels (3.3 million gallons) a day in 1984, placing the state 14th in production in the United States. (Photograph courtesy of BiPetro, Springfield, Illinois)

Fig. 1-1. About 42 percent of the coal produced in Illinois comes from surface mines as shown here in Jackson County. The bulldozer and huge power shovel rest on the coal layer. The power shovel strips the topsoil and rock (the overburden), places it to one side, and exposes the coal seam. (Photograph courtesy of Illinois Coal Association, Springfield, Illinois)

the plants or other organisms on which they fed, are no longer here. Gone forever are the dinosaur, the mammoth, the mastodon, the trilobite, and the tens of thousands of other kinds of land- and sea-dwelling creatures known only from the fossil record (Fig. 1-2). Gone, too, are the broad forests of the 100-foot-tall *Lepidodendron*, the *Sigillaria*, and the *Cordaites* that flourished for a time several hundred million years ago. Fragments of these trees are found today as fossils in certain, appropriately aged sedimentary strata; through the study of them, much has been learned about the Earth's past inhabitants and the varied environments in which they lived.

Illinois has not always been as it is seen today. Nor have its valuable underground coal reserves always been here. They are the products of events that occurred at least 250 million years ago. And Illinois's oil reserves were formed even earlier (Figures 1-3 and 1-4). Its once-flourishing lead- and zinc-mining industries in the northwestern counties (Appendix 1) of Jo Daviess and Carroll center around mineral deposits also formed a few hundred million years ago; the fluorite mining industry in southeastern Illinois and adjacent northern Kentucky centers around mineral deposits that formed perhaps as recently as 100 million years ago. Illinois's fertile prairie soils are based on materials brought here by incredibly huge and thick glacial ice sheets that inexorably but forcefully pushed into this region from the Arctic several times within the past three million years. They carried vast quantities of rock, sand and gravel, clay and silt, and soil from Canada and such northern states as Wisconsin and Michigan. These glacially transported sediments were rearranged and redeposited by meltwater streams and gusty winds that blew off the ice fronts, providing our state with the raw materials to form, in time, some of the richest soil to be found anywhere. Lake Michigan and the other scenic Great Lakes are another legacy of what has come to be called the Pleistocene Ice Ages.

The physical processes associated with the Pleistocene Ice Ages reshaped Illinois on a grand scale. Several times during the past three million years that constitute the Pleistocene Epoch, immense ice sheets invaded Illinois and the other northern states. During most of the past 300 million years, the

Fig. 1-2. A slab of limestone with fossil shells of an extinct brachiopod, *Dicellomus polites*. (Illinois State Museum Collection)

entire Earth, including its polar regions, was free of glacial ice. How and why the several, periodic ice advances and retreats of the Pleistocene developed has been one of the great mysteries of geology, and definite answers are not agreed upon by all who are interested in this question (Fig. 1-5). Recent studies of climates around the world, however, and the systematic probing of the vast Antarctic ice sheet in the southern hemisphere, have confined the explanation to basically an astronomical one. Cyclic variations in the motions of the Earth around the sun and around its own axis clearly triggered the succession of ice advances in the Pleistocene.

Yet to be answered are the questions of how this triggering mechanism operated and why the orbital eccentricities appear to be so strongly impressed on the climatic record of the Pleistocene rather than at other times. Nevertheless, one point stands unchallenged. These glacial masses are still present today in the polar and high mountain regions and have been so for about the past three million years, testifying to how slowly—how incredibly

Fig. 1-3. When accumulated plant materials are buried and compacted, changes may take place that result in the formation of coal. When coal is burned, the sun's energy that was stored in the ancient plant material is released. Illinois's coal is a type called bituminous, the most common kind in the United States; it ranks among the highest in its heat-producing capacity. (Illinois State Museum Collection)

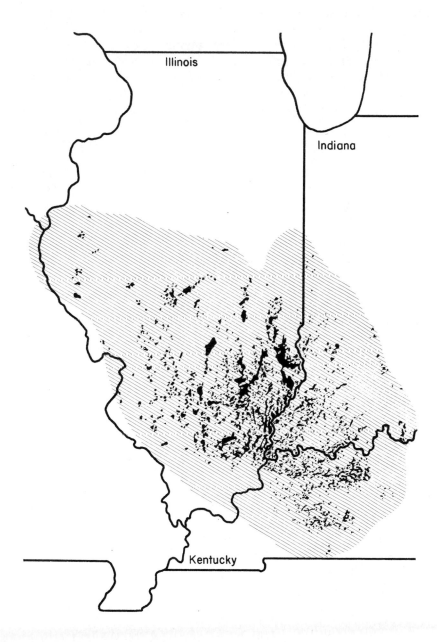

Fig. 1-4. Map of the Illinois Basin of central and southeastern Illinois, southwestern Indiana, and northwestern Kentucky. The basin contains an estimated 340 million barrels of crude oil in known reserves, indicated by the dark patches, with an estimated additional 350 million barrels of undiscovered oil. One barrel equals 42 gallons. (Map courtesy of BiPetro, Springfield, Illinois)

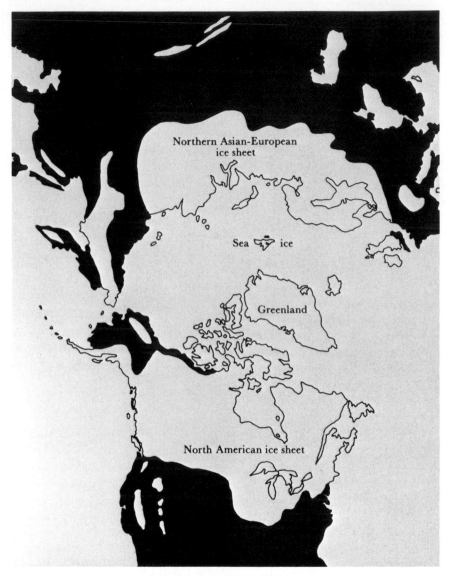

Fig. 1-5. The white areas indicate the extent of land in the Northern Hemisphere covered by glaciers during the Pleistocene Ice Ages. (D. N. Cargo and B. F. Mallory, *Man and His Geologic Environment,* Second Edition, Addison-Wesley Publishing Company, 1977, p. 306, reprinted by permission.)

slowly in the human sense of time—the lands and the climates have changed. But the companions to these Ice Ages glaciers, the mammoth and mastodon, the strange-looking ground sloth, giant beaver, long-horned bison, and long-legged stag moose, as well as almost all the other Ice Ages fauna, are now gone forever from the modern landscape. Their remains, especially of the mastodon and mammoth, are found scattered throughout Illinois and elsewhere in the Midwest.

The geologic story of Illinois is fascinating and will be unfolded here in chronologic order, beginning with the oldest events first. Illinois's terrain lacks the boldness and grandeur of the Rocky Mountains of Colorado, and its rocks the vibrant hues of those seen in the Painted Desert and Grand Canyon of Arizona. Outcroppings of bedrock are not numerous, and many of the landform features developed by glacial activity are not everywhere distinct. But the horizon in central Illinois is endless, the southern unglaciated Shawnee Hills are subdued but stately in their geologic "old age," and the rivers are sweeping and majestic. For a while, Illinois produced more lead than any other state in the Union; today it ranks fifth in coal production. Colorful and impressively large fluorite crystals from Illinois, highly regarded by mineralogists the world over, are found in almost every fine museum collection and prized mineral exhibit (Frontispiece). But to begin immediately with a discussion of the geologic development of our state would be premature. Instead, a discussion of the materials composing the Earth and some of the processes that affect them, is more appropriate.

Chapter 2
Rocks, Minerals, Fossils, and Plate Tectonics

Rocks make up the solid foundation that underlies the surface of the Earth. So varied in composition, texture, and color are rocks that the casual observer often is easily discouraged from trying to learn more about them, especially how they originate and their importance in unraveling past events. This is unfortunate. Lost is the excitement of exploration and discovery that is every prospector's reward. Lost, too, is the opportunity to read geologic history firsthand, because the rocks contain and reveal the record of the Earth's past. Rocks originate in all of the diverse environments that exist on this planet. Therefore, the combinations of temperature, pressure, and chemical interactions within the Earth and upon its surface are many and varied. Such variety in the mineral- and rock-forming processes can make the building of a framework for understanding the nature of rocks a seemingly formidable task. Fortunately, the number of combinations is not limitless, and these result in three basic groups: sedimentary, igneous, and metamorphic.

Sedimentary rock underlies all of Illinois and almost all the Midwest for that matter (Fig. 2-1). It is one of nature's finest examples of the recycling process. Sandstone, shale, and limestone, each a particular kind of sedimentary rock, consist of reconstituted or recycled debris and chemical precipitates that resulted from the natural physical disintegration and chemical decomposition of existing materials in the low-pressure and low-temperature surface environment. Bedrock, when exposed to wind, rain,

Facing page. This imposing cliff, the Modoc Rock Shelter, south of Prairie du Rocher, Randolph County, consists of 350-million-year-old sandstone laid down as soft sand near the shore of a broad sea that covered much of southern Illinois and adjacent lands. Uplift followed by erosion exposed the sandstone. Humans periodically used the protective overhang as a shelter for almost 10,000 years. In 1975, Modoc Rock Shelter was declared a National Historic Site. (Photograph by M. Roos, Illinois State Museum)

snow, and ice undergoes weathering and erosion. It either breaks apart physically to form discrete particles of sediment or decomposes chemically to form soluble compounds, just as sugar dissolves in water. Eventually, the rock and mineral fragments—the sediment—along with the dissolved chemical compounds are carried away by various moving agents that affect the entire surface of the Earth. Running water in streams and rivers is particularly important in this respect, and from the continents, millions of tons of debris are washed into the ocean basins every day. There, waves winnow

Fig. 2-1. Layers of 425-million-year-old limestone exposed in an abandoned quarry at Grafton, Jersey County.

Table 1.
Simple Classification of Sedimentary Rocks

	Clastic Rocks	
Grain Size	Unconsolidated Sediment	Sedimentary Rock
>2 mm	gravel	Conglomerate (rounded gravel) Breccia (angular gravel)
2 to 1/16 mm	sand	Sandstone
1/16 to 1/256 mm	silt	Siltstone
<1/256 mm	clay	Shale

	Chemical Rocks	
Dominant Mineral	Characteristics	Sedimentary Rock
Calcite ($CaCO_3$)	Small crystals	Limestone
Dolomite CaMg $(CO_3)_2$	Small crystals	Dolostone
Quartz (SiO_2)	Smooth, sharp edges	Chert
Halite (NaCl)	Small crystals	Rock Salt

out the finer material, clay and silt mostly, leaving behind beaches of coarser sand with the finer muds and silts settling in the quieter and somewhat deeper water. Under the right circumstances, the dissolved compounds precipitate in the form of chemical materials consisting mostly of calcium carbonate, or lime. Compaction and cementation turn the sediment deposits into layered, sedimentary rock (Table 1). Over 75 percent of the rock exposed at or near the surface of the Earth is sedimentary in origin. It covers the deeper crustal rock which is igneous or metamorphic in origin. In Illinois, the accessible bedrock is only of sedimentary rock; igneous and metamorphic rocks lie buried thousands of feet below the surface.

The multicolored and massive nonsedimentary outcrops seen in the St. François Mountains of the eastern Missouri Ozarks, located about 75 miles south of St. Louis, contrast strikingly with the sedimentary outcrops seen in Illinois (Fig. 2-2). The St. Francois outcrops consist of igneous rocks, which are collections of minerals developed during the cooling of a hot fluid called magma. These form naturally within the Earth under conditions of high temperature and pressure. Igneous rock is the most common material found in the brittle outer layer of the Earth, called the crust. Indeed, the outer 10 miles of the Earth's crust is known to be 95 percent igneous rock that, in most places, is concealed by various thicknesses of sedimentary rock. Igneous rock, although not seen in outcrops in Illinois, is especially important to a better understanding of past geologic events; so much of the Earth's crust is composed of it. The deeper bedrock of Illinois, buried below its sedimentary cover, also consists of this material.

Fig. 2-2. Granite, 1.5 billion years old, exposed in the St. Francois Mountains of the eastern Ozarks at Elephant Rocks State Park. Water flowed into the evenly spaced cracks in the granite and erosion produced the unusual, elephantlike shapes.

All igneous rocks are identified on the basis of composition and texture (Table 2). Only about a dozen minerals are actually involved in determining the composition of an igneous rock. Texture describes the sizes of the minerals present in the igneous rock, which, in turn, reflects the rate of cooling of the mother liquid, that is, the magma. The coarse texture of large minerals reflects a slow rate of cooling; small minerals produce a fine texture, reflecting a quicker rate of cooling.

For instance, granite, one of the common igneous rock types in the St. Francois Mountains, was derived from magma that cooled slowly underground, perhaps over tens of thousands of years. Erosion eventually exposed the coarse-textured rock leaving the granite outcrops seen in the St. Francois Mountains today.

Table 2.
Simple Classification of Igneous Rocks

Texture	Name of Rock			
Coarse (Slow-cooling magma)	Granite	Diorite	Gabbro	Peridotite
Fine (Quick-cooling lava)	Felsite or Rhyolite	Andesite	Basalt	

Composition	Lowest Temperature	Highest Temperature
Predominant minerals common to each of the igneous rocks	Olivine / Augite / Calcium Feldspar / Hornblende / Sodium Feldspar / Potassium Feldspar / Quartz / Mica	

Note: Slow cooling results in rocks with a coarse texture; rapid cooling results in rocks with a fine texture. Differential rates of cooling results in rocks with both coarse and fine textures called a porphyritic texture.

Minerals that make up the granite, seen without magnification, are rich in the elements potassium, sodium, silicon, aluminum, and oxygen, and consist mainly of feldspar, quartz, and mica. When the same type of magma pushes upward to reach the Earth's surface as lava, it cools quickly—in a matter of days, or even hours—to form a fine-textured rock called rhyolite or felsite. These rock types are also seen abundantly in the St. Francois Mountains.

On the other hand, lava consisting mostly of iron, magnesium, and oxygen, that cools quickly at the surface, forms a different kind of igneous rock called basalt, also seen commonly in the St. Francois Mountains. The coarse-grained, slowly cooled equivalent of basalt is gabbro. Other varieties of igneous rock exist in the Earth's crust, and each has been given a name that reflects variations in both the mineral composition and the texture. The general term Intrusive is applied to igneous rock that slowly solidified from magma under high temperature and pressure beneath the surface of the Earth; the term extrusive refers to rock formed from hot material ejected during volcanic activity that solidified quickly on the Earth's surface under low temperature and pressure.

Table 3.
Simple Classification of Metamorphic Rocks

Name	Texture	Foliated or Massive	Minerals Commonly Present
Gneiss	Coarse	Foliated	Quartz, Feldspar, Mica, Hornblende
Schist	Coarse	Foliated	Mica, some Quartz, and Feldspar
Slate	Fine	Foliated	Microscopic Mica, Chlorite, Sericite
Marble	Coarse to fine	Massive	Calcite, Dolomite
Quartzite	Coarse to fine	Massive	Quartz

A third group of rocks results from natural changes that take place when existing rocks and minerals are subjected to high heat, intense pressure, and chemically active fluids at depths of thousands and tens of thousands of feet. Called metamorphic rocks, they owe their particular character to the original composition of the parent material and to the intensity and type of the metamorphosing agents (Table 3). Limestone, for instance, recrystallizes as marble; shale changes either to slate or schist; and granite may be reconstituted as gneiss. Metamorphism often facilitates the development of "new" minerals from the ingredients originally present in the parent rock. For example, garnet, tourmaline, kyanite, and sillimanite are minerals typically developed in a metamorphic environment.

Some of the metamorphic minerals, especially the kyanite and sillimanite, are sensitive to certain temperature and pressure conditions, and this knowledge allows the geologist to reconstruct the nature of the deep crustal environment in which the "new" metamorphic rock formed. Many metamorphic rocks contain flat minerals, such as mica, or needlelike minerals, such as hornblende or tourmaline, all oriented in the same direction. This parallel alignment of the newly formed flat or slender minerals gives the rock a layered appearance called foliation, a property inexperienced prospectors often confuse with stratification, which is universally seen in sedimentary rocks (Fig. 2-3). Slate, schist, and gneiss all display mineral alignment, and these foliated rocks tend to break along the planes of mica, hornblende, or tourmaline concentrations. Quartzite, which is metamorphosed quartz sandstone, and marble, which is metamorphosed limestone, are coarse and granular. Both lack foliation. Little more needs to be said about metamorphic rocks; they are absent both in the subsurface of Illinois and in the St. Francois Mountains.

When studying the different kinds of rock exposed in their natural settings, or "in the field," geologists go beyond simple identification of sandstone, limestone, granite, rhyolite, gneiss, or schist. Each body of rock observed in the field, or recognized through drill core samples, is termed a formation. Formation names are binomial, such as Silvermine Granite, the Dunleith Formation, or St. Peter Sandstone. Geologists note the physical characteristics of the rock unit, whether it is sedimentary, metamorphic, or igneous in origin. If the rock is sedimentary, its position above or below another layer of rock, its thickness, the fossils it may contain, its color, and the trace minerals in it that are recognizable under microscopic observation are also noted. For igneous and metamorphic rock formations, such as the Silvermine Granite, mineral composition is of particular importance. Hundreds of outcrops of the same formation may be seen over many square miles—or only a few hundreds of square feet. The thousands of formations that geologists recognize are the basic framework on which their studies are based.

From this discussion it is evident that familiarity with rocks is incomplete without a better understanding of the nature of minerals. Minerals simply are the building blocks of all rocks (Fig. 2-4). Therefore, the term rock should not be applied to a mineral, nor the other way around. Minerals are chemical compounds of one or more elements, whereas a rock is a physical mixture of one or several kinds of minerals. Granite, for instance, is a rock, an igneous rock; quartz, on the other hand, is a mineral and an important ingredient of granite. Sandstone, too, is a rock, a sedimentary rock, and quartz also is an important ingredient of the sandstone.

Fig. 2-3. Some metamorphic rocks, such as this gneiss, have a layered appearance called foliation caused by the alignment of flat or needlelike minerals.

Fig. 2-4. Rock-forming minerals. *Top, left to right,* quartz, feldspar, and kaolin (clay); *bottom, left to right,* calcite, hornblende, and mica. (Photograph by M. Roos, Illinois State Museum)

From what has been said, then, a rock is a physical mixture of minerals and a mineral is a naturally occurring chemical compound that consists of combinations of various elements. Each mineral present in a rock can be separated from its neighbor by physical means, such as breaking up the rock with a hammer. Each mineral can be placed into a separate little pile that is physically distinguishable from a neighboring pile of a different mineral. On the other hand, the different elements in a mineral cannot be separated physically; they can only be separated by chemical means. The elements, in other words, cannot be separated into distinct piles. Elements are the most basic kinds of matter that occur in the planetary system, and of the 92 naturally occurring elements only seven or eight are so abundant that their chemical characteristics dominate the compositions of almost all minerals.

Two of these elements, oxygen and silicon, are the most important constituents of the Earth's crust, making up about 93 percent of it by volume. Silicon combined with oxygen produces quartz, a glassy looking mineral and the second-most abundant mineral after feldspar, also a silicon- and oxygen-rich mineral. Because of its physical durability in the surface environment, as well as its chemical inertness, quartz is easily recycled and is an important constituent of most sediments, especially sandstone, sandy shale, and sandy limestone. Chemical bonding of silicon and oxygen with several other elements, notably aluminum, iron, calcium, potassium, sodium, and magnesium, produces most of the other common minerals that are so abundant in the Earth's crust. Collectively, these minerals are called silicates.

Only a few rocks lack silicate minerals as major constituents. Limestone, for instance, is a chemical sediment consisting of the mineral calcite, which chemically is calcium carbonate. Dolostone (or dolomite) is composed of the mineral dolomite, similar to calcite but consisting of calcium magnesium carbonate.

Learning to identify just a half dozen minerals, such as quartz, hornblende, augite, calcite, and several different feldspars and micas, allows one to recognize most of the commonly encountered minerals. That is relatively easy. Each of these minerals displays physical characteristics that are readily identified. The real challenge comes from that exciting discovery of the less abundant and the more exotic of the approximately 2,800 other combinations of elements, or minerals, found in nature. The excitement generated from finding these makes mineral collecting an especially popular and stimulating hobby. Add to this the truly magnificent crystal shapes of all minerals, possibly hidden in the dark, rockbound recesses of a mine tunnel or quarry face and therefore rarely found, or the shades and intensities of color unequaled even by the flashiest of flower gardens, and it is understandable why mineral prospecting can become an all-consuming pastime. Exploring for economically valuable mineral deposits, on the other hand, such as lead ore, zinc ore, or fluorite ore, is both essential and challenging, and these activities are among the primary tasks of the geologist (Fig. 2-5).

Past life in the history of Earth is known from the discovery and study of fossils, the remains of organisms buried and preserved in sediments and sedimentary rocks. Fossils consist not only of hard body parts such as bone and shell but also of tracks, trails, feces, and burrows. Paleontology is the science concerned with this fossil record.

Fossils are useful in the reconstruction of ancient environments. Like communities of organisms living today, communities of fossil organisms were adapted to particular environmental conditions. Whether living or fossil, each community is, or was, a dynamic system, mutually dependent and adjusted to a variety of complex influences. The tidal zone along the rockbound coast of Maine, for example, is populated by a distinctly different group of plants and animals than is the softer and sandier shoreline of Lake Michigan. Knowledge of such ecological details of modern environments allows the identification of past environments from the characteristics of the rocks and the kinds of fossils they contain; it is assumed that the natural processes evident today occurred in the same way in the distant geologic past. This is a particularly important assumption and is known as the principle of uniformitarianism, a principle that has played a key role in the development of geology since the latter part of the eighteenth century when it was first expressed. Simply stated, uniformitarianism implies that the forces and processes shaping and affecting the Earth today have always been in operation; thus, a knowledge of present conditions is the key to an understanding of the past. Obviously, present processes include both those that are slow, such as weathering and erosion, and those that are quick and catastrophic, such as volcanism and earthquakes.

Fig. 2-5. Geologist Dr. Richard L. Leary from the Illinois State Museum prospecting near Rock Island in western Illinois and collecting samples of 300-million-year-old shale. Closer examination of the samples in the laboratory helps determine their origin and economic or scientific value. (Photograph by T. Phillips)

Another important conclusion from a systematic study of fossils is that life forms have changed significantly through time. From very simple and limited types of living things found in the older rocks, there followed a progressive development toward more complex and more diverse forms of life in the younger, more recent rocks. Called organic evolution, this concept will be mentioned again later in a discussion about geologic time. Equally important, organisms periodically became extinct, never to reappear in a later geologic time. Knowledge about the evolution of new, younger species and the eventual extinction of older species helps the geologist to place rock units in a particular time frame. Perhaps most important to the geologist is the fact that rock bodies of the same age can be recognized in two or more places, a technique called correlation. While exploring a mountain range in Antarctica, for instance, geologists discovered strata of fossil-rich limestone similar to those seen in the cliffs bordering the Mississippi River in southern Illinois. This discovery indicated that these currently separated regions formed at about the same time in the history of the planet Earth. The fossiliferous limestone strata in both regions formed in almost-identical, warm, subtropical seas. The seas are no longer present at either locality and the climate is no longer subtropical. Correlation of other separated pairs of rock bodies based on their fossil content allows one to reconstruct geography on a continent-wide or worldwide basis at various times in the past.

From geologic studies over the entire surface of the Earth, it is now clear that Earth's history has been punctuated by periods of major igneous activity and mountain building followed by long periods of erosion with the accumulation of sediments. A period of crustal upheaval and magma emplacement is called an orogeny, and the forces accompanying such an event are great enough to squeeze, break, and lift large segments of crust into immense mountain ranges and to compress seemingly brittle and uncompressable rock layers into folds. Upfolds are called anticlines, and downfolds are called synclines. If the stresses are sufficiently intense, the rocks may be broken along faults, and the enormous blocks thus produced may be moved thousands of feet vertically or horizontally. Eventually, these mountain-building forces, these orogenic forces, weaken and stall, and erosion dominates to wear the highlands down. Subsequent burial of a formerly mountainous terrain by the deposition of new sediments, millions of years later, produces an unconformity (Fig. 2-6). Unconformities in the geologic record generally represent missing chapters in the Earth's history because rock strata have been removed by erosion. Nowhere is there a complete rock record spanning all of Earth's history. Earth's rocky crust has experienced many upheavals and subsequent erosion; thus, numerous unconformities characterize the rock record.

Fig. 2-6. This 1.5-billion-year-old granite is overlain by stratified and slightly overhanging 600-million-year-old sandstone at a road cut on U.S. 67 south of Farmington, Missouri, in the St. Francois Mountains. The granite once lay deep in the core of a mountain range and was eventually exposed by erosion. Later it was covered by the much younger sandstone when a shallow sea invaded the region. The boundary between the dissimilar rock bodies is an unconformity, and it represents a missing interval of about one billion years in the rock-building process.

Weaker vertical movements of the Earth's crust, called epeirogeny, produce a gentle uplift or subsidence in response to gravity. Broad uparching of rock produces a structure called a dome, and broad downbuckling of rock produces a basin. Epeirogeny has been the principal force affecting the Midwest as we know it, although several orogenic episodes are known to have taken place in its earliest geologic beginnings. The effect of epeirogenic movements can be dramatic in areas of low relief, especially near sea level. In low coastal environments marine advances, called transgressions, cover the land surface with water. Marine retreats, called regressions, expose more land surface. These events often occur with considerable frequency as the land surface gently rises and subsides in response to the epeirogenic forces.

On an even larger scale, the Earth's crust consists of three major units: continents, volcanic island arcs with their adjacent trenches, and broad ocean basins. Ocean basins alone cover more that 70 percent of the surface of the planet. One obvious difference between two of these major features is that ocean basins are low spots and continents are raised areas. The oceans are floored by dense basaltic rock covered by thin layers of sediment, whereas continents, also covered with various thicknesses of sedimentary strata, are composed mainly of less-dense, granitic material.

Oceanographic surveys involving the systematic mapping of the ocean floors became highly technical and numerous during World War II. Since then, worldwide studies of the ocean basins have revealed some startling facts. A widely held view until the 1940s was that the ocean depths were essentially flat, featureless surfaces. This viewpoint was shattered with the discovery of thousands of submarine volcanoes. Then, researchers found, to their amazement, an oceanic mountain or ridge system that encircles the entire planet like the seams on a baseball. And the volcanic island arcs, such as the Aleutians and the islands of Japan, were found to be bordered by trenches of incredible depths, in one case over 30,000 feet deep. Eventually, a picture emerged of a submersed topographic surface many times more varied and involving formative processes quite different from those shaping the landscapes of the continents.

That discovery, along with observations about the geologic nature of the various ocean-floor features, especially the globe-encircling oceanic mountain system, led to a theory about the origin of the world's oceans based on the idea of sea-floor spreading. This idea is now incorporated in a widely accepted and broader theory called plate tectonics. The theory is quite complex but can be summarized as follows. At the ocean ridge system basaltic magma rises to the surface from deep within the Earth and cools to form new ocean crust. Elsewhere, along certain continental margins and island arcs and deep-sea trenches, ocean crust sinks downward. It flows into the mantle, a 2,000-mile-thick zone beneath the relatively thin 10-mile-thick crust. There, in the upper mantle, the ocean crust remelts into magma. Thus, old ocean crust sinks at the same rate that new oceanic crust is generated at the ridge systems. In a sense, a gigantic conveyorlike system imperceptably carries the new ocean crust, formed at the ridge areas, to the island arcs and adjacent trenches where it remelts in its descent into the mantle. There, in the deeper mantle, the material returns again to the ocean ridge system. Some of the magma generated in the trenches fails to be recycled and rises to the surface, erupting to form the associated volcanic island arcs.

This enormous recycling system is so powerful that it has broken the brittle outer shell of the Earth into about eight large segments, called plates, that move about relative to each other. The forces driving these plates are still not well understood, although immense convection systems as just described are involved (Fig. 2-7). North and South America, for example, are embedded in one plate, the American Plate, like huge logs frozen into a large slab of lake ice. The continents are carried along within these immense plates at modest rates averaging several inches, or as much as a foot or so, each century.

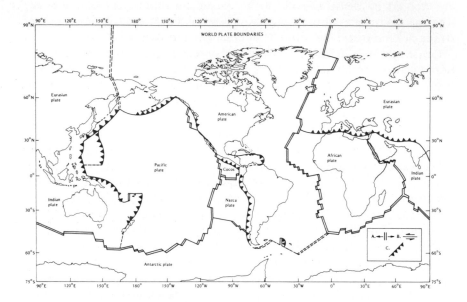

Fig. 2-7. The major plates of the world are separated from each other by narrow boundaries. The plates move apart at mid-ocean ridge boundaries, represented by double lines, **A.** Boundaries where plates slide past each other are shown by single lines, **B.** Trenches and adjacent volcanic island arcs where crust descends into the Earth's interior are marked by lines with teeth on one side that point down the descending plate, **C.** Dotted lines are used where the exact location or character of the boundary is uncertain. (F. J. Sawkins, C. G. Chase, and D. G. Darby, *The Evolving Earth,* Macmillan Publishing Company, 1974, p. 114, reprinted by permission).

According to the plate tectonic theory, the present Atlantic Ocean Basin is geologically quite young; it began to form only about 180 million years ago. At that time, a large, single supercontinent, called Pangaea, developed a series of cracks or rifts along which deep-seated, subcrustal magma began to rise to the surface, wedging the continents apart (Fig. 2-8). Slowly, South America separated from Africa as new emerging crust forced the continents apart, forming the South Atlantic Ocean. A bit later, North America separated from Europe and North Africa as new ocean floor emerged from the Mid-Atlantic Ridge forcing apart these geographic regions and forming the North Atlantic Ocean (Fig. 2-9). Along the leading edge of the westward-moving plate, older ocean crust sank beneath the adjacent plate boundary at the same rate as new crust was forming through volcanic activity along the Mid-Atlantic Ridge. Unseen internal forces were moving the continents about, creating new ocean crust, destroying existing crust, creating mountains and volcanoes, and generating powerful earthquakes renching at the plate boundaries. All these catastrophic activities, past and present, are related to plate tectonics. And as the continents slowly drifted across Earth's different climatic boundaries in response to these subterranean forces, slow but profound changes were taking place in the surface environments and conditions over the millions of years. Antarctica moved from the tropics to the frigid South Pole, and Illinois from the equator to 40° N latitude. The rocks reveal these changes to have occurred; one needs only the skills to read them.

Illinois's current midcontinent position was attained when North America separated from the Old World as the Atlantic Ocean opened up (Fig. 2-10). However, it lay farther east more than a thousand miles and almost on the equator at that time. Illinois continues to drift westward and northward today embedded in the middle of the North American raft, the American Plate, a relatively stable position far removed from the stresses generated along the plate edges (Fig. 2-11). That stability is reflected in the current absence of earthquakes, volcanic activity, and mountain-building episodes, although small Earth tremors occur with some regularity in southern Illinois and adjacent areas to the south in Missouri and Kentucky. Vertical movements in the form of broad epeirogenic warping, both up and down, have been the principal signs of unsteady behavior of the midcontinent for hundreds and hundreds of millions of years.

Illinois's geologic history, then, is contained in its rocks and in its landscapes. These are the legacies of the past. Understanding the geologic processes as they occur today and knowing the kinds of features they produce allows one to interpret conditions that resulted in the ancient sequences of rock. The natural laws have not changed, and the principle of uniformitarianism dictates that knowledge of the present is the key to understanding past events. Fossils provide a valuable record of the development of life forms on this planet. Importantly, the presence of similar fossil assemblages in widely separated sedimentary strata permits the correlation of these strata to the same interval of geologic time. Studying rock bodies, the minerals and fossils they may contain, and the appearance of landscapes, provides the means to reconstruct the complicated series of events that produced them. The remainder of this book will apply such knowledge to "reading" Illinois's rocks and to understanding the evolution of its landscapes.

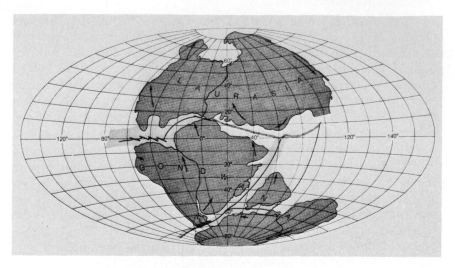

Fig. 2-8. World geography 180 million years ago. After about 20 million years of drift, a super-continent called Pangaea split into a northern landmass called Laurasia and a southern one called Gondwana. New ocean-floor crust is shown as areas shaded gray. Arrows depict the directions of continental movement.

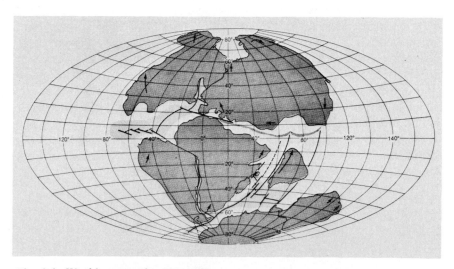

Fig. 2-9. World geography 135 million years ago. North and South America are separating from Africa. The northern Atlantic Ocean is beginning to form as the continents are forced apart.

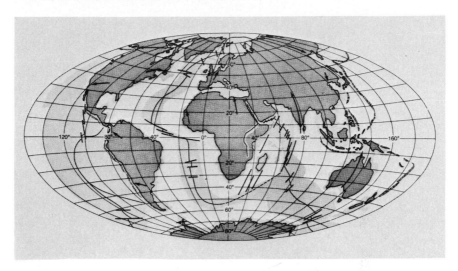

Fig. 2-10. World geography today showing ocean crust produced during the past 65 million years.

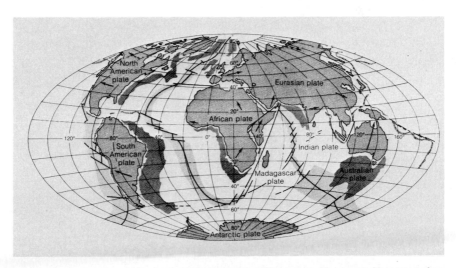

Fig. 2-11. World geography as it might look 50 million years from now if present-day plate movements continue. (Figures 2-8 through 2-11 are taken from *The Breakup of Pangaea* by R. S. Dietz and J. C. Holden. Copyright © 1970. Reproduced by permission of Scientific American, Inc. All rights reserved)

Chapter 3
The Physiographic Regions of Illinois

A land surface is the product of complex interplay among various processes and physical agents that operated in the distant geologic past both on the surface and below. Some of the better-known physical agents that shaped the land through the long course of Earth history include volcanic and earthquake activities; land erosion and sediment deposition by glacial ice, running water, and wind; and the laying down of thick deposits of sediments in ancient lakes or shallow seas, such as is occurring in the Caribbean Sea today.

Erosion of the terrain and accumulation of sediments are surface agents that outwardly reshape the underlying rock foundation of a region. These surface agents are like the hammer and chisel in the hands of a sculptor. Although they outwardly reshape the wood or stone with each blow, the wood or stone itself does not change. The same principle applies to the evolution of a landscape. Whereas the surface changes imperceptively with each rainstorm and with each passing century, the structure of the underlying rock foundation does not change. The term structure, then, has a definite and particular meaning for the geologist. Structure describes the arrangement and the configuration of the rock foundation, or bedrock as it is preferably called. Structure of the bedrock defines the basic and principal differences between various parts of the land surface. By contrast, surface shapes are produced largely by erosion or the deposition of sediments.

Bedrock may be sedimentary, igneous, or metamorphic in origin. Or it may be combinations of all three of these basic rock types. If the bedrock

Facing page. The confluence of the Mississippi River *(left)* with the Ohio River as seen looking north toward Cairo, Illinois. At 268 feet above sea level, this is the lowest elevation in Illinois. The noticeably larger sediment load carried by the Mississippi River is evident by the lighter color of the water. Downstream the two rivers will mix and blend. (Photograph courtesy of Illinois Department of Transportation, Aerial Surveys Division)

consists of sedimentary strata, as is the case in Illinois, it may lie flat like pancakes on a plate. The sedimentary strata exposed in the walls of the Grand Canyon reveal such horizontal structure. Or the rock foundation may have been crumpled, deformed, or fractured by past orogenic movements as happened in the Rocky and Appalachian mountains. Fold and fault structures predominate. The structure may be developed through volcanic activity and consist of extrusive igneous rock as in the Cascade Mountains or Columbia Plateau in the Pacific Northwest. Solidified bodies of intrusive granite, subsequently exposed by erosion, form the structure of the Sierra Nevada of California. In places, the underlying bedrock and its structure may be largely concealed by an uneven thickness of glacially transported boulders, sand and gravel, and clay, as is the case in almost all of Illinois. The bedrock structure, then, seen or unseen, expresses the kinds of physical processes that operated in the past and, when the age of the bedrock is determined, how long ago in its past history these processes were at work.

All the lands of the Earth are part of natural regions. These natural regions are identified principally by the structure of the bedrock that composes each region. Structural differences between each natural region can be further accentuated by differences in climate that govern the processes outwardly reshaping the landscape, such as weathering, and the laying down of sediments by moving water, glacial ice, or wind. When all is said and done, structural differences determine the physical characteristics between natural regions even if the regimes of climate, erosion, and sedimentation patterns are similar.

The United States is divided into 23 natural regions, called physiographic provinces. Each province has a set of descriptive characteristics peculiar to itself and manifests a distinctive framework clearly expressing its structure. For the most part, physiographic provinces are affected by distinctive climates and display particular patterns of vegetation, soil, water, and other resources. Just note how different is the Grand Canyon region of the Colorado Plateau Province in Arizona from that of the Rocky Mountain Province in Montana. Each contains different kinds of bedrock arranged in different structures, is of a different age, and underwent a different course of geologic evolution. A physiographic province, therefore, usually supports a particular economy as well as distinctive cultural traits despite similarities in the outward appearances of cultural features such as motels and banks, billboards and highways, and shopping centers.

Most of Illinois lies in one of the larger of the physiographic provinces in the United States, the Central Lowland (Fig. 3-1). The Central Lowland Province is a vast plain with an underlying structure consisting principally of undeformed, horizontal layers of sedimentary rock. The strata accumulated as soft sand, mud, and lime deposits during periodic invasions of the continent by ancient seas between about 600 million and 300 million

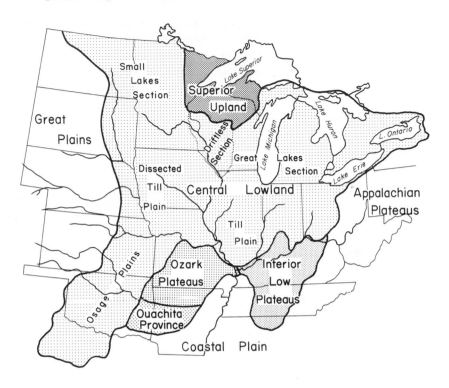

Fig. 3-1. Map of the Central Lowland Province. The Till Plains, Wisconsin Driftless, and Great Lakes sections display distinctive physical characteristics within the Central Lowland Province. Adjoining the Central Lowland Province are the smaller Interior Low Plateaus and Ozark Plateaus provinces, as well as the larger Coastal Plain and Appalachian Plateaus provinces to the south and east, respectively.

years ago. Tens of thousands of feet of sedimentary strata occur here, mostly limestone and shale but some sandstone also, and many of these strata bear rich concentrations of fossil invertebrates. This large plain rises from as low as 500 feet above sea level to as high as 2,500 feet above sea level. It extends from the western half of Ohio in the east to the eastern portions of North and South Dakota, Nebraska, and Kansas in the west. From the Great Lakes in the north it reaches south to east Texas and Oklahoma. Small sections of three other provinces extend across the southern and southwestern borders of Illinois: the Interior Low Plateaus, Ozark Plateaus, and Coastal Plain provinces. To the east of the Central Lowland, beyond Illinois, lies the Appalachian Plateaus Province; to the west the Great Plains Province; and to the north the Superior Upland Province.

Each of the larger physiographic provinces is, in turn, divided into sections. Illinois, along with Indiana and western Ohio, are part of the Till

Plains Section, a particularly large part of the Central Lowland Province that includes more than nine-tenths of the state. Thick glaciers formerly occupied this section, and after melting they left behind a cover of boulders, gravel, sand, and clay that varies in thickness and composition. The term till is applied to a uniform mixture of these materials and its meaning will be more fully defined later in this chapter. In addition to the Till Plains Section, two other sections of the Central Lowland Province extend into Illinois: the Wisconsin Driftless Section in northwestern Illinois and the Great Lakes Section. Only the Shawnee Hills Section in southern Illinois remains as a distinct division, not of the Central Lowland but of the Interior Low Plateaus Province.

In the broadest context, Illinois is a prairie plain, and when compared with other nearby states, it presents little in terms of notable physiographic contrasts. Topographic relief, that is, the differences between high elevations and low elevations, is moderate to slight over most of the state. The highest point, 1,235 feet above sea level, is Charles Mound in the Wisconsin Driftless Section (Fig. 3-2), and the lowest point, 268 feet above sea level, is the junction of the Ohio and Mississippi rivers in the Coastal Plain Province (page 26). These elevational differences provide a total relief of only 967 feet for the state.

Located in the south-central part of the Central Lowland, near the junction of several important river drainages, Illinois is the lowest of the north-central states. Its mean elevation is about 600 feet above sea level, compared with 700 feet for Indiana, 1,050 feet for Wisconsin, 1,100 feet for Iowa, and 800 feet for Missouri. The largest local relief is near the major valleys, within the Wisconsin Driftless Section, and in the Shawnee Hills Section of the Interior Low Plateaus. In these areas, natural rock outcroppings are abundant. These rock outcroppings are especially important in providing opportunities to examine directly the underlying sedimentary rock formations, many of which bear fossils, and to determine the character of their undeformed structure.

Although Illinois lacks large-scale relief, several physiographic regions are evident, and they assume important local significance (Fig. 3-3). The physiographic contrasts between various parts of Illinois are due to several factors and conditions. These include: (1) the topography of the bedrock surface beneath the glacial deposits; (2) the effect of at least two episodes of continent-wide glaciation; (3) differences in topographic features produced by these episodes of glaciation; (4) differences in age of the glacial deposits; (5) the formation of glacial lakes through the natural damming of glacial meltwater; and (6) the absence of glacial deposits entirely.

Illinois's terrain has been profoundly affected by at least two major cycles of sediment deposition brought about by two continent-wide invasions of glacial ice from the northern latitudes. The till and other soil materials left behind by these continental glaciers almost completely conceal

Fig. 3-2. Charles Mound, the highest point in Illinois, is located just below the Wisconsin border in Jo Daviess County, northeast of Galena, Illinois. Barely rising above the surrounding landscape, the 1,235-foot elevation is indicated by the tall, triangular, and isolated Colorado spruce tree in the center of the ridge line.

from surface observation the underlying bedrock and structural foundation in most of Illinois (Fig. 3-4).

Information obtained from the drilling of water and oil wells into and through these glacial deposits reveal that prior to glaciation the Illinois region was an extensive lowland. This broad lowland was developed by erosion of the sedimentary strata that had been laid down mostly under sea water about 300 million years ago over much of what is now central Illinois. While these sedimentary strata lie flat for the most part, in Illinois they have been downwarped epeirogenically to form a basin. This spoon-shaped structure, centered in Illinois, is appropriately known as the Illinois Basin. Bordering it on the north, west, and south were uplands of older and more resistant 500-million-year-old limestone and dolomite strata. Thus, the ancient, preglacial landscape was a low basin in the central region underlain by 300-million-year-old sedimentary rock with higher, more-rugged terrain along the basin edges in the northwest and south underlain by 500-million-year-old sedimentary rock. This is reflected in the shape of the present land surface. The extensive preglacial lowland of central Illinois acquired the thickest accumulations of glacial deposits, and this established conditions for the development of an expansive prairie plain. The uplands on the preglacial basin edges in the Wisconsin Driftless Section and the Shawnee

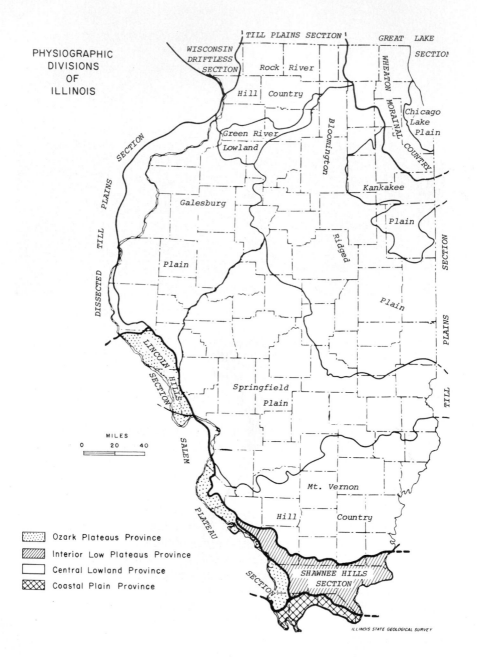

Fig. 3-3. Physiographic map of Illinois outlining the distribution of each of the physiographic sections. (Map courtesy of Illinois State Geological Survey)

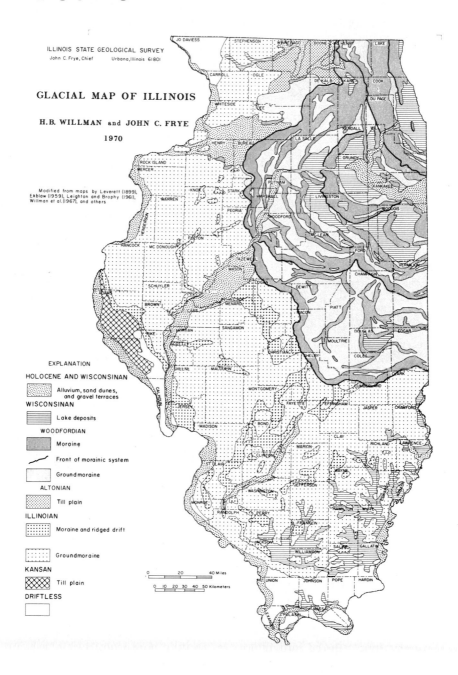

ILLINOIS STATE GEOLOGICAL SURVEY
John C. Frye, Chief   Urbana, Illinois 61801

GLACIAL MAP OF ILLINOIS

H.B. WILLMAN and JOHN C. FRYE

1970

Modified from maps by Leverett (1899),
Ekblaw (1959), Leighton and Brophy (1961),
Willman et al. (1967), and others

EXPLANATION

HOLOCENE AND WISCONSINAN

Alluvium, sand dunes, and gravel terraces

WISCONSINAN

Lake deposits

WOODFORDIAN

Moraine

Front of morainic system

Ground moraine

ALTONIAN

Till plain

ILLINOIAN

Moraine and ridged drift

Groundmoraine

KANSAN

Till plain

DRIFTLESS

Fig. 3-4. Map of Illinois showing the distribution of the major Ice Ages deposits. Ground moraines are less hilly than moraines. (Map courtesy of Illinois State Geological Survey)

Hills Section are thinly veiled or completely free of glacial deposits and stand out in notably rugged contrast and relief.

The most abundant glacial deposits in Illinois were left by the last two of the four known ice advances, first the Illinoian and then the Wisconsinan. A still-older episode of glaciation, the Kansan, is not widely revealed in any of the landscape features, and its deposits are locally restricted to far-western Illinois and portions of southern Illinois. Therefore, the Kansan glaciation will not be considered further. Nor will the even older Nebraskan glaciation.

The four glacial episodes, Wisconsinan, Illinoian, Kansan, and Nebraskan, represent the traditional or classical interpretation of Pleistocene glaciations in North America. Continued studies of the sediment record indicate that additional glaciations, hitherto unrecognized, are involved and a more detailed discussion will follow in Chapter 9.

The Till Plains Section is the area covered by the two most recent episodes of continental glaciation. Till is a term describing unconsolidated sediment deposits, usually neither arranged in stratified layers nor sorted according to particle size. Till was transported into the region by glaciers and then was laid down when the ice melted. When the Illinoian glaciation was at its maximum, nearly 90 percent of Illinois was covered by ice as much as one mile thick, perhaps thicker. At that time the ice touched the higher northern slope of the Shawnee Hills in southern Illinois. This was the farthest southern extent of continental glaciation in all of the Northern Hemisphere, a notable event that occurred about 150,000 years ago.

In Illinois, the Illinoian Till Plain is distinguished by a flatness almost equal to that of a dry lake plain. This flatness is attributed to the fast movement and uniformity of the ice sheet, the leveling action of slopewash, and the low-lying nature of the preglacial Illinois Basin. Slopewash, also called sheet erosion, is the more or less even removal of thin layers of surface sediment from an extensive area of gently sloping land by broad, continuous sheets of running water rather than by streams flowing in well-defined channels. Moraines of Illinoian till interrupt the flatness in local areas. These linear hills of mostly unsorted and unstratified gravel and sand rise 20 to 30 feet above their surroundings, marking the leading edges of the ice fronts. In general, they are poorly preserved, although the Buffalo Hart Moraine of Sangamon County in central Illinois and the Mendon Moraine in Adams County of western Illinois are the more obvious examples (Fig. 3-5).

In contrast to the Illinoian glaciation, the later Wisconsinan glaciation penetrated into only the northeastern quarter of the state (Fig. 3-6). Two major ice lobes flowed into Illinois at the time, one from the Lake Erie Basin to the east and the other from the Lake Michigan Basin to the north. These two ice masses converged in what is now Ford County, near Gibson City in northeastern Illinois. In northeastern Illinois the Wisconsinan glacier developed a succession of moraines, 50 to 100 feet high, a mile or

Fig. 3-5. Isolated, loaf-shaped remnant of the Illinoian Buffalo Hart Moraine seen from Interstate 55 near Elkhart, Logan County, north of Springfield.

two wide, and 50 to 100 miles long. They have a striking concentric pattern that indicates a pulsating retreat and readvance of the ice front (Fig. 3-7). The farthest or outermost edge of this ice front is defined by the north-south-trending Bloomington Morainic System that extends from east of the Rockford area, in the north, to Peoria. South of Peoria, this leading edge is called the Shelbyville Morainic System (Fig. 3-8) and passes near Lincoln, Decatur, and Shelbyville, where it turns eastward through Mattoon and Charleston before leaving the state near Paris in Edgar County. It should be pointed out that the Bloomington Morainic System is considered to be a bit younger than the Shelbyville and that it apparently overrode the Shelbyville Morainic System in northern and western Illinois.

The recognizable effects of these two episodes of continental glaciation cannot be understated. The Wisconsin Driftless Section, of which more will be said shortly, was untouched by either the Illinoian or Wisconsinan ice sheets. Also left untouched was the Shawnee Hills Section. Both display a bolder, sharper topography with more relief; here the thin soils lack glacial till and rock outcroppings are numerous. The Rock River Hill Country and Mount Vernon Hill Country, on the other hand, are characterized by gently rolling, subdued hills with thin veils of Illinoian till (Fig. 3-9). Each lies adjacent to an unglaciated terrain and each occurs along the distant edges of the Illinoian ice sheet. Their present land surfaces partially reflect a

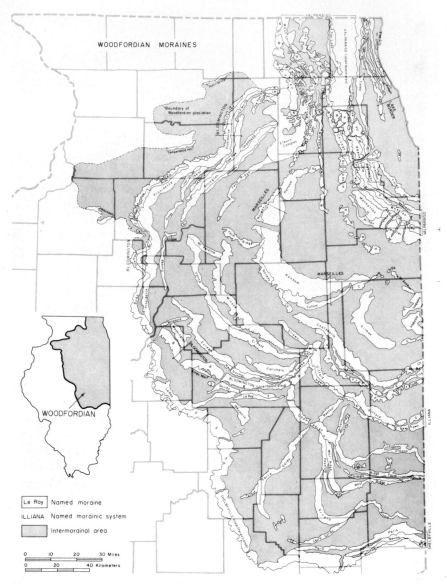

Fig. 3-6. Map of northeastern Illinois showing the moraines of Wisconsinan age.
(Map courtesy of Illinois State Geological Survey)

Fig. 3-7. Moraine Hills State Park at McHenry, McHenry County, illustrating the hilly and rolling character of the Wisconsinan moraines.

Fig. 3-8. Driving north along Interstate 55 near Atlanta, Logan County, a traveler drives up the Shelbyville Moraine from the flatness of the Illinoian Till Plain.

preglacial bedrock of low relief that was only slightly modified and subdued by a cover of thin till. By observing these landscape characteristics, it is clearly evident that a topographic revolution took place in Illinois as a consequence of the continent-wide invasions of glacial ice, a revolution that resulted in a general leveling of a formerly more rugged landscape.

The successive superposition of younger till sheets upon older ones in some parts of Illinois and the deposition of only one till sheet in other areas produced additional contrasts in the present topography. A landscape dominated by the underlying bedrock characterizes both the Mount Vernon Hill Country and the Rock River Hill Country. This is due, in part, to both these regions having only one cover of glacial till, the Illinoian. Glaciated areas elsewhere in the state, such as the Bloomington Ridged Plain, Kankakee Plain, and Wheaton Morainal Country were buried beneath at least two till sheets, the Illinoian and Wisconsinan, and possibly the Kansan and the still older Nebraskan as well.

Two contrasting Wisconsinan glacial topographic features—the Wheaton Morainal Country and the Bloomington Ridged Plain—strongly illustrate the differences in glacial landforms evident in the state. The Wheaton Morainal Country lies in the Great Lakes Section. It is distinguished from

Fig. 3-9. The view west along Route 20 in the Rock River Hill Country Section of Stephenson County. This area is a few miles east of the Wisconsin Driftless Section. Although a glaciated area, the Rock River Hill Country has comparatively thin till deposits that fail to mask the rolling character of the preglacial topography.

the Till Plains Section by the bold, concentric moraines of the Lake Michigan Basin, the greater prominence of lakes, and the extent of former glacial lakes in this area. Ice lobes, confined to constrictions imposed by the deep Lake Michigan Basin, resulted in the formation of closely grouped moraines. In molding the Bloomington Ridged Plain, on the other hand, the Wisconsinan glacier was much less confined and more widely radiating, and during its many stages of recession and readvance, it formed a conspicuous series of more widely spaced concentric morainal ridges. These alternate with nearly featureless till plains that lie between the moraines, moraines that generally are smoother than the more bold, more closely spaced, and more roughly contoured moraines of the Wheaton Morainal Country.

The Till Plains Section has areas of different physiography and these clearly reflect the contrasting ages and characteristics of each of the two major till deposits found here. The outer, western edge of the Bloomington Ridged Plain, for example, defines the boundary between the younger tills of Wisconsinan age to the east from the older Illinoian tills present in the Galesburg Plain and the Springfield Plain to the west and south. The Mount Vernon Hill Country still farther south is also underlain by Illinoian till. The younger Wisconsinan glaciation produced the pronounced morainal landscape of the Bloomington Ridged Plain; the greater age of the Springfield and the Galesburg plains and the Mount Vernon Hill Country farther south, all composed of Illinoian till, is reflected by the general absence of pronounced morainal features in these areas. These latter landscapes are older and eroded, showing a more mature aspect in their landscape features.

The Springfield Plain includes the level Illinoian till sheet in central and south-central Illinois (Fig. 3-10). It has a more shallowly entrenched drainage system as compared with the more sharply incised valleys of the Galesburg Plain. Elevation above the main lines of drainage is the prominent difference between the Galesburg Plain and Springfield Plain. The surface of the Galesburg Plain stands higher above the Illinois River so that its valleys are more sharply incised than are those of the Springfield Plain (Fig. 3-11).

Although most of the Springfield Plain is flat, moraines are more conspicuous in its western part than elsewhere on the Illinoian till. They include the Mendon and Buffalo Hart moraines, as well as an extensive area of ridged till on the Kaskaskia drainage basin in the southwestern corner. The topography developed in this older till sheet is in marked contrast to that just described for the Bloomington Ridged Plain and Wheaton Morainal Country of Wisconsinan age. The Illinoian surface is older, its morainal features are more subdued, its till deposits have undergone longer and deeper weathering and erosion, and its drainage pattern is more integrated and organized.

Fig. 3-10. The Springfield Till Plain is a level expanse, as seen in this view looking west from Interstate 55 near Pawnee, Sangamon County. Crude oil pumped to the surface is from a 385-million-year-old reservoir rock about 2,000 feet below the surface.

Unlike the physiographic regions described so far, the Chicago Lake Plain and the Kankakee Plain owe their physiographic characteristics not mainly to till deposits but rather to glacial meltwater lake and meltwater stream deposits. The Chicago Lake Plain is a flat surface sloping gently toward present Lake Michigan. This plain, the well-known featureless "prairie" of early writers of the area, is interspersed by low beach ridges, morainic headlands and islands, and two large glacial meltwater drainageways along the Des Plaines River and Sag Channel. During Wisconsinan time, the present Great Lakes were even larger than they are today with the larger Lake Chicago being the forerunner of Lake Michigan. As the Wisconsinan glacier withdrew, an expanding Lake Chicago was eventually impounded between the retreating ice and the Valparaiso Morainic System, which is the system of moraines in the Chicago area. The glacial discharge eroded the outlet channel along the Des Plaines Valley.

With further retreat of the ice beyond the Straits of Mackinac linking Lakes Michigan and Huron, a lower outlet emerged. This lower outlet reversed the drainage of Lake Chicago and permitted drainage eastward through Lakes Huron, Erie, and Ontario and the St. Lawrence Valley into the Atlantic Ocean. With the disappearance of Lake Chicago, the Chicago Lake Plain emerged. Beach ridges, sand spits, and sand bars were formed by wave action along the shore; these parallel the lake shore or trend southwestward toward the outlet channel along the Des Plaines River. Blue Island, a prominent morainic island, is located just east of the outlet channel and rises about 50 feet above the lake plain. Sand dunes, which are so conspicuous along the present lakeshore farther to the east, scarcely are recognizable here and are found in only a few scattered localities.

The Kankakee Plain, separated from the Chicago Lake Plain by the Wheaton Morainal System, also was formerly occupied by not one but several glacial lakes, including Lakes Wauponsee and Watseka. These lakes may have been present for 500 to 1,500 years. The Kankakee Plain differs from the Chicago Lake Plain in that the lakes that covered it were not part of glacial Lake Chicago, the forerunner of modern Lake Michigan, but were instead temporary expansions of the numerous glacial floods that occurred during the melting of the Wisconsinan glacier.

Finally, the Green River Lowland is a low, poorly drained plain dominated by sand ridges and dunes. Over 100 feet of glacial sediments have been deposited in this area. These were carried into a preglacial lowland by streams draining through the Bloomington Morainal System. Evidence suggests that at this time almost all of northeastern Illinois drained into the lowland. The glacial lakes provided places for additional sediments to accumulate. Remnants of the older Illinoian moraines are evident at Harrisville in northeastern Ogle and southeastern Winnebago counties, at Temperance Hill in the center of Lee County, and at Atkinson in

Fig. 3-11. The Spoon River valley is deeply incised into the Galesburg Plain. This is a view east from the western bluffs of the valley on Interstate 74 in Knox County.

east-central Henry County. Some of the sand ridges in the Green River Lowland are, in part, bars developed on the stream-washed outwash surface, but many are true wind-blown dunes.

Perhaps the most intriguing physiographic region of the Central Lowland Province is the Wisconsin Driftless Section. Drift is a general term that describes all glacial deposits, a more inclusive term than "till." The Wisconsin Driftless Section is an area of approximately 20,000 square miles, lying mostly in Wisconsin, with no recognizable glacial deposits. All evidence seems to indicate that none of the continental ice sheets reached this area. It is an "island" surrounded by a terrain buried beneath Wisconsinan, Illinoian, and possibly even older ice sheets.

Why the Wisconsin Driftless Section was ice-free is not easily explained. Perhaps its location partway between the deep valleys and basins of Lakes Superior and Michigan may have been a factor. The ice sheets may have been funnelled into and channelled through the deeper valleys and basins leaving insufficient ice to spill into the Driftless Area. Or perhaps its location on the leeward, south side of the higher, protecting ridges in the Superior Upland Province may have been a factor. The highlands deflected the ice sheets around this region.

Evidence that the Wisconsin Driftless Section escaped glaciation is strong. Most notable is the lack of both glacial deposits and modified features, such as glacial striae. Striae are scratches on bedrock surfaces produced when rock debris carried beneath and within the glacier acts as grit, much like sandpaper rubbed over balsa wood. Such striae are seen in rock outcroppings outside the Driftless Section (Figures 3-12 and 3-13).

On a larger scale are the picturesque rockscapes seen, for instance, at the Wisconsin Dells north of Madison (Fig. 3-14). These consist of especially fragile features, such as natural bridges and arches, and isolated buttes, rock towers, and spires that resemble pins ready to be bowled over by the next glacial advance. None of these landforms could have survived had they been overridden by glacial ice. Less obvious, but evident nevertheless, are the stream-drainage patterns in this section. Pronounced valleys indicate a well-established and well-integrated pattern that has not been rearranged by glacial erosion or blocked and interrupted by glacial deposits. The drainage displays a well-defined dendritic pattern, like the venation in a leaf, with the smaller valleys narrow and noticeably V-shaped in profile. Rock exposures are numerous. In the Illinois portion of the Driftless Section, these consist mainly of 500-million-year-old dolomite and limestone that border the Mississippi River Valley in a magnificent and bold line of cliffs such as those seen at the Mississippi Palisades State Park north of Savanna in Carroll County (Fig. 5-5). Indeed, a significant lead and zinc industry flourished in the region from the late 1700s through the mid-1900s, and Galena, in Joe Daviess County, for a time between 1820 and 1865 was the most important producer of lead in the nation (Fig. 3-15). The ore was extracted largely

Fig. 3-12. Shallow striations and deeper gouges cover the surface of this Pennsylvanian-aged sandy dolomite exposed southeast of Lake Springfield, Sangamon County. Rock debris carried by the Illinoian glacier between 125,000 to 500,000 years ago produced these markings. The pencil points out the southwestern trend of the striations.

Fig. 3-13. Two sets of glacial striations are etched into Pennsylvanian-aged limestone at a quarry near Fairmont, Vermilion County. One set trends S 20° W, the other trends S 40° W. Each indicates that the region was overridden two times during the Wisconsinan glaciation between about 75,000 and 10,000 years ago. Finely pulverized clay and silt (called rock flour) produced a smooth, mirrorlike polish that is still evident after many thousands of years. (Photograph courtesy of Illinois State Geological Survey)

Fig. 3-14. A rock spire of 550-million-year-old sandstone stands isolated along the shore of the Wisconsin River in the Wisconsin Dells. Such fragile landforms could not have survived the impact of the mile-high glaciers that covered the surrounding region. (Photograph courtesy of the Wisconsin Division of Tourism)

from surface diggings into the easily accessible, unglaciated dolomite and limestone outcroppings. Mills processed the lead which then was sent down the Galena River to the Mississippi and onward to southern ports such as St. Louis, Missouri.

As pointed out earlier, the terrain of the Wisconsin Driftless Section is considerably rougher than the adjacent Rock River Hill Country. Conspicuous landforms that rise above the general surface are referred to as mounds. These mounds stand out boldly because of their height, their steep slopes, and their heavier growth of timber. The majority, such as Charles

Fig. 3-15. This crevice mine was dug during the early 1800s into a dolomite cliff overlooking the Mississippi River near Galena, Jo Daviess County. Dozens of these shallow mines were cut into the 480-million-year-old dolomite. The miners were searching for lead ore and their tunnels are called the "California Diggings."

Mound, the highest elevation in Illinois, are irregular in shape, flat on top, and not uniform in slope. They rise 100 to 200 feet above the general surface and cover areas ranging up to one-quarter mile square. The lower slopes are steeper than the average lower slopes of the surrounding region, and slopes in the upper 15 or 20 feet of elevation are commonly vertical, or nearly so. Some of the better-known mounds are Horseshoe, Dygerts, Scales, Hudson, Mount Summer, and, of course, Charles Mound (Fig. 3-16). The bases of the mounds are softer shales; these are capped and thereby preserved by a much harder dolomite. In such a situation, the upper slopes remain steep because the soft shales erode more quickly than the dolomite cap.

South of the Till Plains Section and southeast of Illinois lies a broad and greatly elongated northeast-southwest-trending domal structure called the Cincinnati Arch. This arch is the principal structural feature of the Interior Low Plateaus. It stands between the Appalachian Plateaus still farther to the east and the Illinois Basin to the north and west. Lying almost entirely within Illinois, the Illinois Basin is a broad structural downfold of the Central Lowland Province, and this structural feature, as mentioned, underlies the surface glacial cover. The topographically bold western portion of the Interior Low Plateaus Province is identified as the Shawnee Hills Section, which somewhat confusingly is called the "Illinois Ozarks." This area is **unrelated to the Ozark Plateaus Province centered in Missouri. A pro-**

nounced topographic change marks the northern border of this section where it is in contact with the topographically less-varied till deposits of the Mount Vernon Hill Country. The northern edge of the Shawnee Hills is defined by a robust, deeply dissected, and fairly steep escarpment consisting of hard, resistant, and northerly dipping sandstone strata about 300 million years old. The presence of this almost 800-foot-high escarpment was perhaps to some degree responsible in preventing the Illinoian ice sheet from penetrating farther into this southern portion of the state and in this way may have served as a topographic barrier.

South of the escarpment, the Shawnee Hills consist of a deeply dissected, lower-elevation plateau underlain mostly by northerly dipping older sandstone and shale (Fig. 3-17). The southern boundary follows the northern edge of the overlapping and younger sedimentary strata of the Coastal Plain Province that dip gently to the south. The western edge of the Shawnee Hills

Fig. 3-16. Dygerts Mound *(left)* and Pilot Knob *(distant right)* typify the terrain of the Wisconsin Driftless Area in Jo Daviess County a few miles south of Galena, Illinois.

is drawn somewhat arbitrarily along a boundary where uplift has been sufficiently strong to bring to the surface the still-older rock strata of the Ozark Plateaus Province. This eastern segment of the Ozark Plateaus, containing limestone formations 400 million to 500 million years old, is called the Salem Plateau Section.

The Ozark Plateaus Province, an area of about 40,000 square miles west of the Mississippi River and south of the Missouri, consists of a broad,

Fig. 3-17. Camel Rock in the Garden of the Gods of the Shawnee Hills Section south of Harrisburg, Saline County, is one of the best-known scenic landmarks in Illinois. Its 300-million-year-old sandstone has been weathered and eroded along evenly spaced vertical joints and the horizontal stratification. Over hundreds of centuries it has acquired the shape of a camel.

asymmetric, domal uplift, much like the Cincinnati Arch already described. It has been unevenly dissected by stream erosion and is surrounded by lowlands. Because this asymmetric dome slopes more steeply on the east than it does on the west, it is higher in Missouri than elsewhere. Subsequent erosion of the dome has exposed some of the oldest rocks evident in the Midwest. These are igneous in origin, and they occur in the St. Francois Mountains (Fig. 3-18).

The Salem Plateau Section of this province extends into the southwestern corner of Illinois. This section is not identified on the basis of any marked topographic change in Illinois but rather is recognized primarily on the basis of its geology. Limestones of about 350 million and 400 million years of age underlie the Salem Plateau. The only portion of the Ozark Plateaus Province lying within Illinois is the bold limestone bluffs that marks the edge of the Mississippi Valley.

Confusingly, the robust topography identified with the unglaciated Shawnee Hills in southern Illinois often is identified as the "Illinois Ozarks." But the "Illinois Ozarks," as pointed out earlier, lie

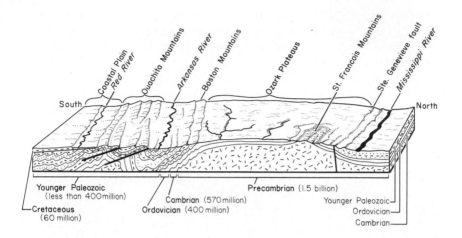

Fig. 3-18. The Ozark Plateaus extend from the Mississippi River below St. Louis to the Coastal Plain Province in northern Texas, a distance of about 300 miles. The Ozark Plateaus Section is a structural dome consisting of 600- to 500-million-year-old sedimentary strata overlying 1.5-billion-year-old igneous rock. This older, Precambrian igneous rock is exposed in the St. Francois Mountains. (C. B. Hunt, *Natural Regions of the United States and Canada,* W. H. Freeman and Company, 1974, p. 346, reprinted by permission)

within the Interior Low Plateaus Section rather than the topographically higher, more dissected, and geologically older Ozark Plateaus of Missouri.

The Coastal Plain in Illinois includes the southernmost tip of the state and is underlain by particularly soft and poorly consolidated young sediments about 60 million years old. These overlap the older sedimentary strata in the Shawnee Hills. The Cache Valley, which was the ancient Ohio River Valley at one time, sharply separates the Shawnee Hills from the Coastal Plain Province. Unlike the other sedimentary rock formations described so far, these dip toward the south rather than to the north. Included in this province are the broad alluvial plains of the Cache and Mississippi river valleys and the hills between the Cache and Ohio river valleys. These alluvial plains are characterized by terraces and recent floodplain features, such as short, abandoned, U-shaped stretches of the river called oxbows, or oxbow lakes. Horseshoe Lake in Alexander County is a well-known example (Fig. 3-19).

Clearly, Illinois's topography has been shaped and reshaped many times by a variety of geologic processes. Over thousands, millions, and hundreds of millions of years—even more than a billion years—these processes, both at the surface and below it, relentlessly altered the shape and look of the land. To reconstruct the most distant geologic events for which a record is known, it is necessary to turn back the hands of time no less than 1.5 billion years. The geologic record from that time lies, however, concealed for the most part beneath younger layers of sedimentary rock. But it is not inaccessible everywhere. Extensive exposures of this ancient rock occur in the St. Francois Mountains. And drill core samples have been obtained in Illinois. Although limited in distribution, the preserved record from this earliest beginning reveals events both geologically exciting and unique to the Midwest. Dramatic events dominated the opening chapter in Illinois's geologic evolution—profoundly physical events that were not to be repeated again in the future.

Fig. 3-19. Horseshoe Lake at Olive Branch, Alexander County, is an abandoned meander loop of the Mississippi River. Today, it attracts thousands of overwintering Canada geese that are managed by the Illinois Department of Conservation. Bald cypress and tupelo trees give the area a "southern" character. This scene is part of a life-sized habitat display at the Illinois State Museum. (Illinois State Museum Collection)

Chapter 4
1.5 Billion Years Ago:
Volcanoes Shape the Land

Geologists prefer not to speak of events in the Earth's history in terms of so many thousands, millions, hundreds of millions, or perhaps billions of years ago, even though the chapters here are titled in this way. Instead, they speak of an event as having occurred in a particular time interval, such as the Precambrian Era, or the Devonian Period, or the Pleistocene Epoch.

It has long been known—for almost 200 years—that Earth history could be separated into intervals of relative or nonnumerical time. One of the first of these nonnumerical time references was a simple classification of rocks into Primary, Transition, Secondary, and Tertiary ages. The oldest rocks were designated as Primary and the youngest as Tertiary. Before the discovery of radioactivity in 1896, and the subsequent development of radioisotopic dating methods in the early 1900s, the assigning of numerical ages to rocks and to past geologic events was not possible. Only a non-numerical or relative system of time reference could be established. Relative time expresses all past events in relationships to each other and in chronologic order. Relative time identifies one event occurring before or after another event. For instance, a layer of sandstone is older than a layer of shale that lies above it, and the Transition age predates the Secondary.

Central to the recognition of relative time is the now well-known fact that during the long course of Earth history different kinds of animals and plants lived on its lands and in its seas. Many of these organisms have disappeared forever and are known today only by their fossils. Evolution of new kinds of plants and animals and the extinction of existing ones are normal events recognized by a study of the fossil record. The extinction of a species

Facing page. Precambrian, metamorphic quartzite, about 1.5 billion years old, is preserved in delicate rock spires in the Baraboo Range of the Wisconsin Driftless Area north of Madison, Wisconsin. Devil's Lake is in the background. Rock of this age is not seen at the surface in Illinois but is known from well records.

of plant or a species of animal is not as exceptional an event as many persons might like to think. Hundreds of thousands of species of animals and plants evolved and then vanished from the lands and seas of the Earth during the long course of history. In addition, a study of fossils indicates that through evolution organisms tended to become progressively more complex with time. This progression of evolution and extinction of plant and animal species provides a guideline to divide the Earth's past history into distinct time segments. Thus, episodes of relative geologic time are recognized simply by the similarities—or the differences—of the groups of fossils that occurred at the same time or at different times in the Earth's past history. The most commonly used segment of relative geologic time recognized by the kinds of fossils contained in the sedimentary strata is called a Period. Periods may be subdivided into Epochs, and related periods are grouped into a larger segment of time called an Era.

The first signs of probable life appear in the sedimentary rocks from the early Precambrian Era. These are found in South Africa and Australia. Through radioisotopic dating methods, the rocks are calculated to be about 3.5 billion years old. Evidence obtained recently in Antarctica indicates that life may have first appeared even earlier, about 3.8 billion years ago; the Earth itself is thought to be between 4.5 to 5 billion years old. These earliest fossils are extremely small and, when seen under the microscope, resemble simple bacteria and single-celled algae. From these initial beginnings, life evolved slowly in the seas for more than three billion years. Those early organisms were soft-bodied, lacking the hard parts necessary for preservation, and are therefore especially rare as fossils. This general absence of fossils makes it difficult to chronologically organize the events of the Precambrian Era. But about 600 million years ago a variety of complex invertebrate organisms, with hard and preservable exoskeletons, suddenly appeared for the first time in the fossil record (Fig. 4-1). Included are invertebrates as complex in their anatomy and physiology as the trilobites. This event suggests some drastic changes in the environment at this time and marks the end of the four-billion-years-long Precambrian Era and the beginning of the Paleozoic. Following the Precambrian, geologic time is separated into three eras: the Paleozoic or the time of primitive life; the Mesozoic or the time of middle or transitional life; and the Cenozoic or the time of recent and more modern-looking life forms. Seven periods of geologic time divide the Paleozoic Era; beginning with the oldest, these are the Cambrian, followed by the Ordovician, Silurian, Devonian, Mississippian, Pennsylvanian, and Permian. Three periods divide the Mesozoic, and again beginning with the oldest, these are the Triassic, Jurassic, and Cretaceous. Two periods divide the Cenozoic Era, the older Tertiary and the younger Quaternary.

Figure 4-2 lists these divisions of geologic time in what is called a geologic column, that is, a summary of both the kinds of rocks and the units of

Fig. 4-1. These fossil trilobites, *Calymene celebra,* occur in Silurian dolomite exposed in a quarry at Grafton, Jersey County *(Fig. 2-1).* Trilobites are complex, marine invertebrates, and their sudden appearance in early Cambrian rock implies a lengthy evolutionary development during the late Precambrian, from which time few fossils are known. (Photograph by M. Roos, Illinois State Museum)

relative geologic time that make up Earth history. A geologic column lists all time units starting with the oldest, the Precambrian Era, at the base and continuing up to the present, the Holocene Epoch of the Quaternary Period of the Cenozoic Era, at the top. A local geologic column lists only those rocks and time units that occur in a specific area, such as a state or a county. The geologic column illustrated here is the standard for North America.

It is apparent that a large section of the geologic record is missing in Illinois. Illinois has no rocks at or close to the surface that originated in the Precambrian. That is not to say that Precambrian rocks do not occur here. Rock materials of the Precambrian are found at depth: 20 samples, mostly granite, have been collected from cores drilled over 2,000 feet beneath the surface in northern and western Illinois; farther south and east, in the heart of the Illinois Basin, Precambrian rock is found more than 17,000 feet below the surface. Extensive outcroppings of Precambrian rock, on the other hand, are seen at the surface in eastern Missouri, in the particularly scenic and mineralogically interesting St. Francois Mountains of the Ozark Plateaus Province mentioned in the previous chapter.

Rocks of Permian, Triassic, or Jurassic age, however, are nowhere evident in Illinois, even in the deep subsurface. Nor are they seen elsewhere in the Midwest, for that matter, although some evidence for the Permian is thought to exist in Kansas and Nebraska. And only a few, thin strata from the late Cretaceous Period are preserved in the Coastal Plain Province of southern Illinois and also in west-central Illinois. This is somewhat unfortunate because the Triassic, Jurassic, and Cretaceous periods are well known as the famous "Age of Reptiles" when fierce-looking dinosaurs,

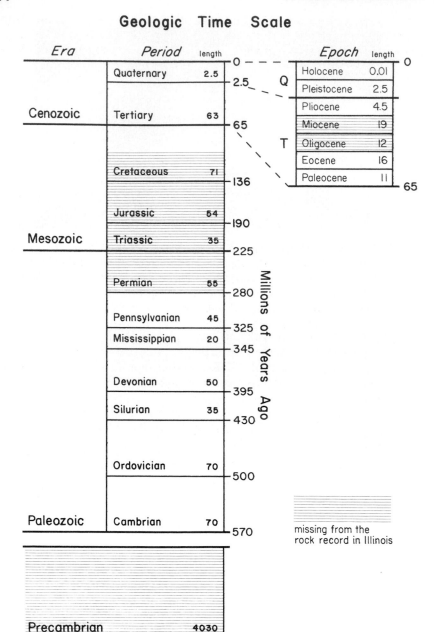

Fig. 4-2. The geologic time scale for North America showing the approximate age and duration of each era, period, and epoch. The ages are in millions of years. Periods and epochs missing in Illinois are shaded. Fossils preserved in sedimentary rock establish relative age, such as Silurian Period or Pleistocene Epoch. (Illustration courtesy of J. King, Illinois State Museum)

gigantic marine reptiles, and gliding reptiles were the dominant life-forms on Earth. Since rocks of the Mesozoic Era are mostly absent in the Midwest, fossils of sauropods and theropods, ichthyosaurs and mosasaurs, and pterosaurs and other saurians have not been found in Illinois.

In the St. Francois Mountains ancient Precambrian rocks are seen at the surface. They are easily accessible for studying and reconstructing the physical events that occurred in the region at this time (Fig. 4-3). Illinois is not so fortunate because Precambrian rock can be obtained only by drilling. Granite and two principal kinds of volcanic rock, felsite and felsite porphyry, have been recovered by drill cores in Illinois. Radiometric age determinations indicate these rocks to be between 1.4 and 1.1 billion years old, the same age as those exposed at the surface in the St. Francois Mountains. In Illinois, deposition of Cambrian-age sediment began not much more than 525 million years ago; the unconformity on the Precambrian igneous rocks represents a lost interval spanning between 600 to 900 million years in length for which little is known (Fig. 2-6). By studying core samples from rocks more than one billion years old, especially those seen in outcrop in the more than 1,000 square miles of the St. Francois Mountains, a generalized geologic history of this time period can be reconstructed.

The physical events that occurred during the Precambrian were especially dramatic, and the rock record reflects a time in the physical evolution of the midcontinent, including Illinois, that was not to be repeated. Majestic

Fig. 4-3. Precambrian rhyolite porphyry *(foreground)* is exposed at the top of Knob Lick Mountain between Farmington and Fredericktown in the St. Francois Mountains. Relatively "softer" Precambrian granite underlies The Flatwoods beyond, an area of relatively low relief; the higher hills on the horizon are composed of the more resistant, volcanic rhyolite, felsite, and felsite-rhyolite porphyries. These volcanic rocks resulted when silica-rich magma erupted cataclysmically and dissolved gases held under pressure within the magma exploded upon reaching the surface.

volcanoes dotted the landscape for hundreds, even thousands of miles, volcanoes as inspiring in their symmetry, stature, and activity as are the snow-covered and glacier-scarred volcanoes of the Cascades in Oregon and Washington today. The nature of the rocks, especially the felsites and felsite porphyries, suggests that superheated ash, dust, and gas erupted in powerful, roaring blasts similar to the awesome 18 May 1980 eruption of Mount St. Helens (Fig. 4-4). Felsites and felsite porphyries form in this way

Fig. 4-4. In Washington, Mount St. Helens reawakened with terrible suddenness in the spring of 1980. Volcanologists calculated that the force of this explosion was one of the largest in the conterminous United States in the last two centuries; the energy released was equivalent to 10 million tons of TNT. Such explosive eruptions, historical ones and those from the geologic past, have a high-silica magma in which gases are trapped. The build-up of stupendous pressure produces dense, incandescent clouds of superheated ash and suspended gases that roll downhill in fiery, turbulent avalanches at initial speeds of 300 miles per hour. Felsite, rhyolite, and related porphyries result when such incredibly explosive eruptions occur. This Mount St. Helens scene, with its 60,000-foot-high eruptive plume, is reminiscent of the Midwest 1.5 billion years ago when hundreds of volcanoes were undergoing similar eruptions. (Photograph courtesy of United States Geological Survey, Department of the Interior)

Fig. 4-5. Top-grade granité from Elephant Rocks State Park near Graniteville, Missouri. Known around the country as "Missouri Red," the granite blocks were left behind when quarrying stopped. Salmon-pink feldspar colors the granite, giving the rock its commercial name. The granite, about 1.2 billion years old, takes a high polish and was used for tombstones and building stone. One of the oldest, this granite quarry opened about 1845, furnishing stone for the famous Eads Bridge that spans the Mississippi River at St. Louis and for the cobbles in the city's streets. Granite from quarries in this area was used in the Marshall Field Building in Chicago and in major buildings in New Orleans, Dallas, Baltimore, San Francisco, Pittsburgh, and other large cities in the United States. The Thomas Allan monument in Pittsfield, Massachusetts, is a single, polished column of "Missouri Red," 42 feet high and 4 feet square at the base.

today—at Mount St. Helens, Krakatoa in the straits of Java, and Mount Pelee on the island of Martinique in the Lesser Antilles, to mention only three particularly well-known eruptions. These present-day and easy-to-witness volcanic events help to interpret more accurately the now silent Precambrian record that is our far distant geologic heritage.

Volcanic quiescence followed this long period of activity and growth. The shattered cones, vestiges of their former selves, stood as silent monuments to that earlier episode of upheaval. In time, they were deeply eroded, perhaps destroyed altogether, only to be rebuilt during a second phase of intense and violent volcanic activity several hundred million years later, now about one billion years ago. Massive intrusions of granite subsequently invaded these newer—as well as older—volcanic rocks, the magma perhaps lacking the force to pour out onto the Precambrian surface before it cooled and solidified at depth (Fig. 4-5). Erosion again followed, long and deep, this time uncovering much of the deeply formed granite and producing a mountainous terrain of granite and felsite with a relief estimated to be in excess of 1,000 feet.

At the same time, in the distant seas unaffected by these dramatic events, life was beginning, evolving, diversifying, and becoming ever more complexly structured. Algal masses, simple jellyfishlike forms, primitive worms, and other soft-bodied organisms appeared at this time, although the fossil record is exceedingly scarce. Nothing lived on the lands. No plants nor animals, not even insects, lived in the valleys and mountains, on the plains and plateaus, or on the volcanic cones. The land was a uniformly gray, reddish-brown, and brown wasteland—stark, barren, and empty. Only the ferocious blasts and powerful shock waves from the erupting volcanoes shattered the unearthly stillness.

Although the Precambrian land surface may have been barren, two rich mineralizing events were occurring far underground at this time. First, heavy concentrations of valuable iron in the forms of hematite and magnetite were being created, and later, deposits of exploitable silver, lead, and tungsten were formed. Iron has been produced for more than 150 years in the St. Francois Mountains and was a strategically important mineral resource during the Civil War (Fig. 4-6). Shepherd Mountain, Pilot Knob,

Fig. 4-6. Pilot Knob Mountain, as seen from Fort Davidson, Missouri. The "notch" in the mountain top is where magnetite ore was removed by open-pit mining. Ore piles from recent, deep, underground mining are seen in the foreground and at left. The Pilot Knob Pellet Company recently abandoned the mining and milling of this still-rich ore body.

Fig. 4-7. This entrance to the Einstein Silver Mine near Fredericktown, Missouri, is about 50 feet above the St. Francis River. The tunnel is a horizontal approach, called an adit, to the ore-bearing vein, and was known as the "River Tunnel."

and Iron Mountain, all located near Arcadia, Missouri, provided almost all of the ore for this effort. Indeed, on 26 and 27 September 1864, the battle of Pilot Knob was waged, and in a brief span of 20 minutes, more than 1,000 officers and men lay wounded and dying at the foot of Pilot Knob Mountain at Fort Davidson. The Confederate objective? To destroy the St. Louis and Iron Mountain Railroad that was used by the Union forces to haul iron ore to St. Louis.

Silver mining began nearby in 1877, and by the mid-1880s, when the mines closed, a modest 3,000 ounces of silver, 50 tons of lead, and some traces of gold were produced (Fig. 4-7). Silver-bearing lead sulfide, technically called argentiferous galena, was the source of the silver. The silver mines reopened in 1916, not for silver but this time for the tungsten obtained from such tungstate minerals as wolframite and scheelite (Fig. 4-8). Probably not more than several hundred tons of tungsten ore was processed, a particularly rare strategic material, during the years of World War I and II. Today, the mining town is gone, and oak and pine trees grow where miners and their families once walked the streets (Fig. 4-9). But the

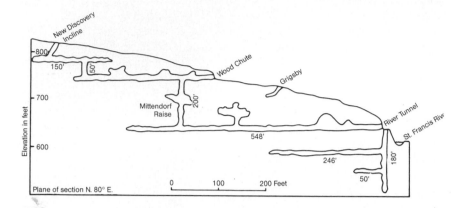

Fig. 4-8. As this diagrammatic cross section of the Einstein Silver Mine shows, the River Tunnel adit followed the vein for a distance of 548 feet. A 180-foot-deep incline was sunk near the entrance to reach the ore. Two other levels were opened above the River Tunnel, and it was formerly possible to ascend to the top of the hill through the underground workings and exit through the New Discovery Incline. The width of the ore zone varied; it probably was not over seven feet maximum width with the richest concentration being only two feet wide. (Diagram courtesy of Missouri Department of Natural Resources, Division of Geology and Land Survey)

Fig. 4-9. The Einstein Silver Mine area circa 1895. The view is to the north; the St. Francis River flows south. The large boulders and outcrops are Precambrian granite. Buildings on the western bank of the river were constructed for milling and processing ore. Note the dam in the distance; a portion still stands today. At the height of mining activity, when 200 or 300 miners were employed by the company, the population of the town was between 800 and 900 persons. (Photograph courtesy of Missouri Department of Natural Resources, Division of Geology and Land Survey Archives)

ore piles still can be found in what today is the Silver Mines Recreation Area in the Mark Twain National Forest, and with patience and persistence one can uncover excellent specimens of argentiferous galena, wolframite, scheelite, zinnwaldite, cassiterite, fluorite, arsenopyrite, and other minerals. The mine tunnels still can be seen, and the dam, built across the St. Francis River to drive a turbine wheel, still stands. Here is to be experienced first-hand that close encounter with those rare specimens that make mineral collecting—"rockhounding" as it is popularly called—such an exciting and rewarding pastime (Fig. 4-10). The exposed Precambrian bedrock in the St. Francois Mountains is located at the eastern edge and is structurally the highest uplift of the Ozark Dome. Long-term and deep erosion has exposed to view a small section of the crystalline basement that forms the fundamental and underlying foundation of the midcontinent (Fig. 3-18). These mountains of mainly extrusive and intrusive igneous rock can be likened to a little window into the cellar of the continent. Beyond the St. Francois Mountains, the basement lies largely concealed in the dark and remote recesses of Earth's interior, buried beneath a cover of Paleozoic and younger sedimentary materials; in Illinois, these mineralogically rich and varied Precambrian granites, felsites, and felsite porphyries lie everywhere buried.

Fig. 4-10. These rockhounds are collecting silver-bearing galena and the tungstate minerals scheelite and wolframite at the Einstein Silver Mine. The River Tunnel adit *(Fig. 4-7)* is at the foot of the ore pile.

Chapter 5
600 Million Years Ago:
Time of Tropical Seas

Over the stark and barren Precambrian landscape, a distant sea began a slow advance from the south. The once majestic volcanoes, reduced by erosion to merely rugged hills, became islands, and by 525 million years ago they were submerged under the deepening sea. As this late Cambrian sea advanced northward, a thickening blanket of sand was deposited over the Precambrian intrusive granites and volcanic felsites. Detailed studies of the resulting sandstones indicate that the land sources for these sediments were from the north, northeast, and east; little sediment appears to have been derived from the Ozarks to the west. Well-rounded quartz grains and a minor amount of heavy minerals such as hornblende and magnetite compose the different sandstones. The sand for these early Paleozoic sandstones appears to have been derived from erosion of nearby Precambrian highlands, transported oceanward by streams and deposited in the steadily advancing and deepening Cambrian sea. Outcrops of the sandstones, the first known record since the Precambrian, are not common in Illinois, although these sandstones underlie all of the state (Figures 5-1 and 5-2). Small outcrops occur in Ogle and Lee counties, and Cambrian sandstones directly underlie the thick glacial drift in Lee and DeKalb counties where they occur on the south, or upthrown side of a northwest-southeast-trending fault known as the Sandwich Fault. Elsewhere, Cambrian rocks range in thickness from about 1,000 feet in the subsurface in southwestern Illinois to more than 3,400 feet in the eastern part of the state.

By late Cambrian time, Illinois was part of a broad sea, far from any shore and far from the sources of clastic sediments. During Ordovician time the sediments deposited were mainly chemical precipitates—limestone and

Facing page. A high-pressure water hose is used to hydraulically mine the Ordovician-aged St. Peter Sandstone Formation in a large, open quarry at Ottawa, La Salle County. This pure quartz sandstone is used in several commercial industries, including the manufacture of glass.

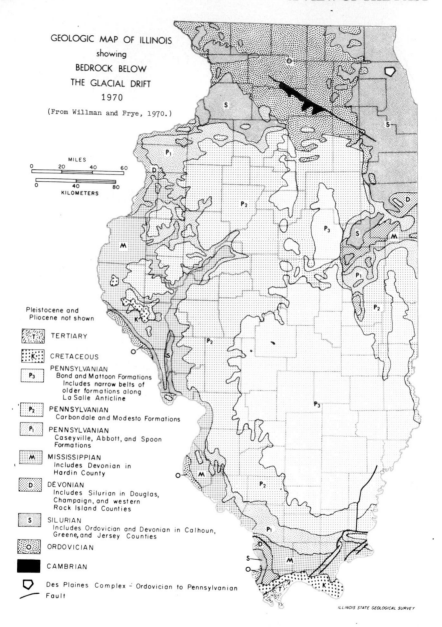

GEOLOGIC MAP OF ILLINOIS
showing
BEDROCK BELOW
THE GLACIAL DRIFT
1970

(From Willman and Frye, 1970.)

MILES
0   20   40   60
0   40   80
KILOMETERS

Pleistocene and
Pliocene not shown

TERTIARY

CRETACEOUS

PENNSYLVANIAN
   Bond and Mattoon Formations
   Includes narrow belts of
   older formations along
   La Salle Anticline

PENNSYLVANIAN
   Carbondale and Modesto Formations

PENNSYLVANIAN
   Caseyville, Abbott, and Spoon
   Formations

MISSISSIPPIAN
   Includes Devonian in
   Hardin County

DEVONIAN
   Includes Silurian in Douglas,
   Champaign, and western
   Rock Island Counties

SILURIAN
   Includes Ordovician and Devonian in Calhoun,
   Greene, and Jersey Counties

ORDOVICIAN

CAMBRIAN

Des Plaines Complex - Ordovician to Pennsylvanian
Fault

ILLINOIS STATE GEOLOGICAL SURVEY

Fig. 5-1. Geologic map of Illinois. The youngest Pennsylvanian strata, **P-3**, lie in southeastern Illinois and are surrounded by progressively older strata. Such an age distribution, with the youngest strata in the center and progressively older strata in the surrounding area, results from the broad downwarp of the Illinois Basin. The much younger Cretaceous and Tertiary strata are not part of this broad basin structure but overlap the basin from the Mississippi Embayment of the Coastal Plain. (Map courtesy of Illinois State Geological Survey)

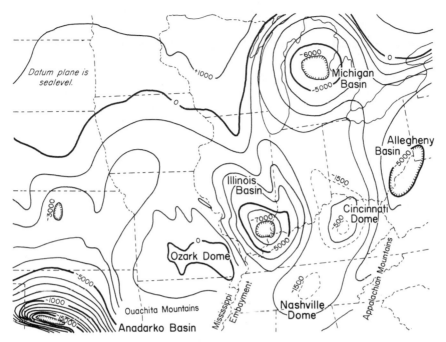

Fig. 5-2. This structure map of Cambrian strata allows one to "see" below the ground surface to the top of the Cambrian strata, which in southeastern Illinois lie over 7,000 feet underground. In north-central Illinois, they appear near the surface; in south-central Wisconsin they are broadly exposed. Note the following structures revealed by a circular or elliptical shape in the contours: Illinois Basin; Michigan Basin; Ozark Dome; Cincinnati Dome; Nashville Dome; Allegheny Basin; and the pronounced Anadarko Basin in western Oklahoma where the Cambrian strata are more than 19,000 feet below the surface. A structure-contour map of this kind is especially useful in oil exploration because it helps locate oil-bearing strata of a particular kind or age.

dolomite. Late in the Ordovician Period, as the first distant tremors of the soon-to-be-born Appalachian Mountains a thousand miles to the east were being felt, clastic sediments of clay and silt were swept into the Ordovician sea of Illinois. These accumulated above the earlier limestone and dolomite. Large deltas pushed westward from the newly born and rising Taconic, Green, and other young mountain ranges in eastern America, and the sediments forming these deltas were washed into the late Ordovician sea of Illinois.

A temporary withdrawal of the sea followed by a brief cycle of erosion and then a readvance of the sea during mid-Ordovician time resulted in the deposition of a significant, and today commercially valuable, sandstone, the St. Peter Sandstone Formation. This formation is exposed along the

Illinois and Fox rivers near Ottawa; the Rock River and Castle Rock State
Park near Oregon; at Starved Rock State Park; and along the Mississippi
River near West Point Landing in Calhoun County (Fig. 5-3). Impressive
outcroppings are also seen in Matthiessen State Park near LaSalle and along
the highway between Dixon and Oregon where the sandstone has been eroded into particularly scenic bluffs and canyons. The St. Peter Sandstone Formation varies from only a few feet to more than 700 feet in thickness but
commonly is 100 to 200 feet thick. It consists largely of fine- to medium-
sized, well-sorted, well-rounded, and distinctively frosted grains of weakly
cemented quartz sand; the sandstone easily disintegrates into individual
quartz grains by the mere rub of the hand over its surface. The St. Peter
Sandstone Formation is composed of exceptionally pure quartz sand, free
from such impurities as clay, silt, carbonate minerals of calcite and
dolomite, iron, and the miscellaneous heavier minerals that are common to
most sandstones. No fossils, except for occasional worm borings, have been
found in this sandstone. It was laid down as a beach deposit, that is, a near-
shore sand accumulation in which the individual quartz sand grains were
continuously agitated and moved about with each breaking wave of the sea

Fig. 5-3. Ordovician-aged St. Peter Sandstone is exposed in the 125-foot-high
Starved Rock butte along the Illinois River near Utica, La Salle County. Legend re-
counts that in the 1760s a band of Illiniwek Indians was trapped and took refuge on
top of this outcrop. Surrounded by hostile Ottawa-Potawatomi tribes, they eventually starved. (Photograph courtesy of Illinois Department of Conservation)

that had advanced northward through Illinois. Quartz grains on modern beaches characteristically are frosted as they abrade each other with each breaking wave; the St. Peter Sandstone must, therefore, be a prehistoric beach deposit. Where it occurs today in Illinois is where the ancient mid-Ordovician shoreline had stood.

Sandstone of the St. Peter Sandstone Formation is a commercially important source of silica sand. The Illinois silica sand industry centers around Ottawa, Wedron, Troy Grove, and Utica in LaSalle County, and in Oregon in Ogle County. Two principal grades of silica sand are produced—washed and crude. For some uses it is not necessary to remove the minor impurities, but for other uses the sand is washed. The washed silica sand produced in Illinois has many uses, and its suitability for specific purposes depends in part on its having been screened to specific sizes.

The purity of Illinois washed silica sand makes it desirable for making glass, a product which is more than half silica sand. Each year more than a million tons are used for this purpose. The purity of the sand also is of importance for chemical and metallurgical uses, such as the manufacture of sodium silicate and silicon carbide, and in alloying. The hardness of the sand makes it useful for grinding large sheets of plate glass to prepare them for polishing and also makes it an effective abrasive agent for sandblasting. Metal casting in foundries and the exteriors of buildings are cleaned by this process. Illinois produces thousands of tons of sand each year for such abrasive purposes.

Because the coarser grains of the washed silica sand are rounded, strong, and available in uniform sizes, oil-drill operators use thousands of tons of it annually in the hydraulic fracturing of oil-bearing strata. The sand is mixed with oil, other petroleum products, or water, and is forced by powerful pumps into the sandstone or limestone formations containing oil. The great force thus exerted opens fractures in the rock strata and pushes the liquid and sand into them. When the pressure is relieved, the sand grains serve as props to hold the fractures open. Oil can then flow more easily into the wells and production is increased.

The washed sand is clean, and being chemically inert it is used to filter impurities from drinking water. Its whiteness makes it a desirable constituent in plaster, mortar, and precast building panels. Being able to withstand high temperatures without melting, the washed silica sand is used to make molds into which molten metal is poured to make various kinds of castings. A special type of coarse silica sand from Illinois is carefully prepared to be of uniform grain size. This is used throughout the world as a standard in laboratories that test cement and other commercial products. Some silica sand is ground to a fine, white powder. The powder, called ground quartz, ground silica, silica flour, or potter's flint, has many uses. It is an ingredient in paints and enamels, in making pottery and china, in scouring powders, and in making molds used for precision metal castings.

On the other hand, unwashed or crude silica sand generally is yellow or yellowish-white. Originally white, the sand grains are coated by iron oxide, similar to the rust that forms on iron. Thousands of tons of crude silica sand are mined annually. Because it is highly heat resistant, much of it is bought by foundries to make molds used for casting, especially steel castings, of automobile engine blocks, train wheels, and a variety of other metal products. Crude silica sand also is used to seal cracks and openings in industrial furnaces to prevent the loss of heat; in certain ceramic products; and for adjusting the silica content in Portland cement.

Illinois remained almost continuously beneath the sea during Silurian time, and, as was the case during most of the Ordovician Period, the strata deposited were predominately carbonates—dolomite in the northern part of the state and largely limestone, siltstone, and shale in the southern part. The most striking feature in the Silurian seas, however, was the development of extensive coral reefs. A broad area of reefs at this time reached from the Ozark region northeastward across Illinois, Indiana, Ohio, western New York, and northern Ontario (Fig. 5-4). These reefs are impressive both in size and extent. They supported a wide variety of marine invertebrates in much the same way as do the modern coral reefs of the South Pacific and the Great Barrier Reef of Australia. The Silurian reefs of Illinois contain a wide variety of corals, bryozoans, brachiopods, crinoids and other marine-dwelling invertebrates.

Silurian strata are well exposed in the Mississippi River bluffs from Jo Daviess County southward to the vicinity of Rock Island (Fig. 5-5). They also are exposed in the Mississippi and Illinois river bluffs in Jersey and Calhoun counties. On the other hand, in southern Illinois, Silurian exposures are limited to the Mississippi bluffs and tributary valleys in Alexander County and southern Union County.

Sedimentation continued into Devonian time; however, withdrawal of the seas and minor epeirogenic uplift resulted in the absence of Devonian strata in some parts of Illinois. And by the later part of the Devonian, muddy sediments rich in plant spores as well as fine organic debris were being deposited in the relatively deep seas in the southern part of the Illinois Basin. They formed a black, thinly laminated, and easy-to-split shale. Conditions favoring this type of sedimentation were widespread during the late Devonian, and black sediments covered almost the entire basin at this time. Devonian strata, however, are limited in their outcrop areas and are seen principally along and near the Mississippi and Ohio river valleys.

Some of the Devonian strata, especially the Clear Creek Chert Formation, have been chemically altered into an extremely fine-grained, or microcrystalline, form of silica, known commercially as tripoli. Alexander County in southern Illinois produces most of this material (Fig. 5-6). The powdery tripoli is used for many purposes, such as preparing abrasives, paint fillers, scouring compounds, metal polishes, fiberglass, silicone rub-

Fig. 5-4. This coral reef flourished in the Silurian sea and is reconstructed on the basis of fossil evidence. Corals, such as the large, rounded reef-building tabulates, were especially common. So, too, were the flower-shaped, filter-feeding crinoids and blastoids. Small, shell-bearing brachiopods cover the surface of the reef. Several trilobites try to escape from the taper-shaped, tentacle-bearing nautiloid cephalopods that were the primary predators on the reef. As in modern coral reefs, the organisms living during Silurian time were bright and colorful. (Photograph courtesy of Milwaukee Public Museum)

ber, billiard cue chalk, and electrical resistors. Elsewhere, tripoli is produced only in Oklahoma, Missouri, and Pennsylvania. It consists chiefly of minute particles of microcrystalline quartz held firmly together. Although the origin of tripoli is speculative, the original rock is thought to have consisted of siliceous limestone and calcareous chert. Interbedded within the limestone strata were layers of chert containing various amounts of calcite. As these rocks were exposed to surface weathering, water percolated downward into the cracks and crevices, gradually removing the more soluble calcareous material. After many hundreds of thousands of years, all the soluble calcite was removed, leaving behind a microcrystalline "skeleton" of the less soluble quartz particles to form the tripoli deposits recognized today.

Marine limestones again dominated the rock record during Mississippian time, an indication of the return of a broad, deep, warm sea and a clearing of the formerly muddy waters. Many of these limestones are not only thick but are exceedingly fossiliferous, perhaps more so than any of the previous rock formations discussed so far (Fig. 5-7). Brachiopods are par-

Fig. 5-5. Majestic bluffs overlook the Mississippi River and Iowa at Mississippi Palisades State Park north of Savanna, Carroll County. The view is to the south. Silurian dolomite underlies the bluffs.

Fig. 5-6. Abandoned tripoli pit in the Devonian Bailey Limestone near Olive Branch, Alexander County. The chert-bearing limestone has been silicified by a natural but not well understood process.

Fig. 5-7. Fossil specimens of **1.** the screwlike bryozoa, *Archimedes,* **2.** two bud-shaped, filter-feeding blastoids, *Pentremites,* **3.** a long-hinged, spiriferid brachiopod, and **4.** a dome-shaped, productid brachiopod. These fossils, and others, typically occur in Mississippian limestone formations. (Illinois State Museum Collection)

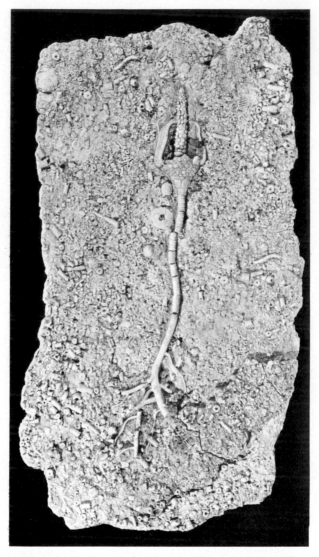

Fig. 5-8. A nearly complete fossil crinoid with a flowerlike "head" (calyx), a stem
that consists of hundreds of individual washerlike disks, and a holdfast or "root."
Notice the numerous broken pieces of crinoid stems and individual stem disks in the
limestone slab. (Illinois State Museum Collection)

ticularly numerous, with spirifirids and productids, two distinctive and
easy-to-identify kinds, being most abundant. The Burlington Limestone,
and to a lesser extent the overlying Keokuk Limestone, consist almost entirely of crinoid debris (Figures 5-8 and 5-9). Fenestrate bryozoan
fragments, mostly of the corkscrew-shaped *Archimedes*, are especially
abundant in some of the limestone layers. Blastoids, particularly the pen-

Fig. 5-9. Reconstruction of a crinoid. Crinoids and blastoids *(Figures 5-7 and 5-8)* resemble plants because of their flowerlike calyses, stems, and rootlike holdfasts. They are bottom-dwelling filter-feeders and members of the spiny-skinned echinoderms, as are the modern sea urchin and sand dollar. (Illinois State Museum Collection)

tremitids, are characteristic of other limestones formed at this time. Shark teeth also are common in some beds of the Burlington and Keokuk limestones. These Mississippian strata are well developed in the Illinois Basin south of a line running roughly from Monmouth, Warren County, to Hoopeston, Vermilion County. Welldrill cores reveal that the Mississippian strata are more than 3,200 feet thick in southern Illinois, near the deepest point of the Illinois Basin.

Although limestone is the dominant rock type in the Mississippian System, a large siltstone delta developed in what is today central and eastern Illinois. Shale and sandstone formations are prominent in this part of the state. The main source for these clastic sediments appears to have been

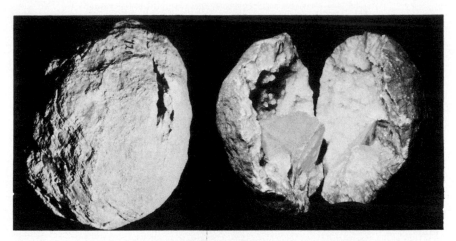

Fig. 5-10. This geode specimen *(left)* was collected near Warsaw, Hancock County. Until the geode was opened *(right)*, there was no evidence that the interior space was lined with hundreds of small-bladed crystals of calcite. (Illinois State Museum Collection)

northeast of Illinois, and a broadening delta grew southwestward into the sea of the Illinois Basin in the later part of the Mississippian Period. The ancient Michigan River flowing southward from Canada across Michigan, a corner of Indiana, and into Illinois, transported considerable sand and silt into the sea by means of an ever-lengthening and ever-widening delta. Alternation of limestone and sandstone formations resulted from lateral shifts in the mouth of the river and in the position of the shoreline during the progressive sinking of the basin.

Any discussion of the Mississippian System of rocks would be incomplete without reference to the world-famous quartz geodes found near Warsaw, Illinois, in Hancock County, and at Keokuk, Iowa, on the opposite side of the Mississippi River (Fig. 5-10). Geodes are rounded masses of mineral matter, hollow on the inside, with a base layer that supports clusters of well-formed and numerous, inward-pointing crystals of various sizes. Those from this area are of exceptional beauty and are eagerly sought by almost everyone with even the most passing interest in minerals and crystals. When broken open the base layer or interior lining of the Warsaw-Keokuk geodes is seen to consist of a type of quartz known as chalcedony, or cryptocrystalline quartz. The inward-pointing crystals sparkle brightly in the light and usually consist of beautiful, hexagon-shaped, and pointed crystals of quartz. Calcite, pyrite, barite, and the crystals of other minerals may also be present to line the interior of the geode.

The rock bodies in which geodes occur are limestone, especially those layers in the lower part of the Warsaw Formation (Fig. 5-11). Usually the size of a baseball or a grapefruit, the geodes developed within the limestone host rock after the limy sediment was laid down. One explanation of how these crystal-lined nodules formed is that the geode previously was merely a tiny, pea-sized cavern, either formed by limestone solution, or representing the original small cavity between the two adjoining shells of a brachiopod or other shelled marine invertebrate. In either case, subsequent changes in the physical and chemical conditions within the sediment layer resulted in an increased differential pressure within the cavity. This cavity ultimately was enlarged by the increased pressure, and the harder lining material of the growing cavity pushed aside the surrounding softer limy sediment. The enlarged cavity then was lined with calcite crystals and noncrystal calcite, both precipitated from the lime-saturated water slowly moving through the enlarged cavity. In time, quartz chalcedony replaced the calcite lining, and then, later, crystal quartz replaced the original calcite crystals to fill the cavity. Crystal growth proceeded inward, from the outer margin of the cavity toward the center; therefore, the interior crystals are younger than those

Fig. 5-11. The geode-bearing Warsaw Formation is exposed in this quarry near Hamilton, Hancock County. The geodes occur as elliptical masses, especially near the top of the outcrop. (Photograph courtesy of Illinois State Geological Survey)

on the outer margin of the cavity. It is not uncommon for crystals to completely fill a cavity, thereby producing a solid rather than a hollow geode.
Erosion eventually removed the surrounding limestone, leaving behind the
sphere of harder and more-resistant chalcedony and quartz crystal-lined
cavity either on the surface of the ground or visibly exposed in the outcrop
face. Why the Warsaw Formation was affected in this way has not been
answered, an unsolved mystery that in no way detracts from the beauty of
these much-prized Warsaw-Keokuk geodes.

Fig. 5-12. The mineral galena, from which lead is extracted. (Illinois State Museum
Collection)

    In the mid-seventeenth century, the French became firmly entrenched
in the eastern Great Lakes region and began to look westward toward the
Illinois country for a route leading to the Gulf Coast. During this period of
exploration, they paid keen attention to reports of deposits of economically
valuable metals and minerals. Although they discovered no gold or silver,
they did find extensive deposits of lead in the Upper Mississippi Valley
region (Fig. 5-12). Two major sources of the lead-bearing mineral, called
galena, appear on early eighteenth-century maps. One was in the Upper
Mississippi Valley region encompassing contiguous portions of present-day
Iowa, Illinois, and Wisconsin in the Wisconsin Driftless Section. The other
was along the Meramac River, a tributary to the Mississippi River, in the St.
Francois Mountains.

The French, and others thereafter, mined the lead. By 1820 and on through 1865, the Upper Mississippi Valley mining region achieved the distinction of being the nation's principal source of lead ore. Peak production was reached between 1845 to 1847 when the annual output was reported at 27,000 tons of lead metal. As the known richer and shallower deposits were depleted, as market conditions changed, and as various factors adversely affected the supply of miners—including their departure in the famous California Gold Rush of 1849—lead mining declined substantially to a fraction of its former importance. Zinc, mined almost exclusively from the larger, deeper, and less-accessible deposits of the mineral sphalerite, replaced lead as the chief metal product of the region beginning around 1860 (Fig. 5-13). With reserves exceeding those of lead, zinc production peaked during World War I when 64,000 tons of zinc metal were produced in 1917. This fell to 6,000 tons in 1921 (Fig. 5-14).

Fluctuations in the production of economic minerals both in Illinois and elsewhere is not unusual. The mining of base metals such as lead and zinc has always been an unstable business, and zinc production from the Upper Mississippi Valley Mining District has waxed and waned primarily in response to economic controls rather than resource availability. Over 300 years of continuous mining activity in the Upper Mississippi Valley—one of the longest in the United States—ended on 1 October 1979 with the closing of the District's last operating mine at Shullsburg, Wisconsin. Although large quantities of ore remain to be extracted from the region, it is uncertain if and when production will ever again be considered a profitable venture.

Studies of the lead and zinc ore deposits reveal that they occur in mid-Ordovician dolomites; in northwestern Illinois, as well as in adjacent Wisconsin and Iowa, these dolomites make up the older Platteville and overlying Galena formations (Fig. 5-15). While the lead ores occur in strata of mid-Ordovician age, it is known that these valuable mineral deposits did not form during Ordovician time but sometime thereafter; the lead and zinc ore bodies show clear evidence of having penetrated the already-formed Ordovician dolomites. But exactly when the ore minerals formed is a matter of dispute. Some geologists suggest that the lead- and zinc-mineralizing event occurred after Silurian time, perhaps around the Pennsylvanian Period when the Appalachian Mountains in eastern America were beginning to form and the structural effects of this distant mountain-building episode were felt in the Illinois Basin. Others assume the mineralizing event was of igneous origin, suggesting instead a possible Cretaceous age on the basis of dates on some igneous dikes evident in Kentucky and Arkansas. Still others suggest that the event occurred as recently as the Tertiary Period. The point, however, is that although the time of the mineralizing event is debatable—anytime between the late Paleozoic to early Cenozoic—the galena and sphalerite concentrations occur only in dolomites of mid-Ordovician age.

Fig. 5-13. This rock sample contains two minerals: white calcite and sphalerite, the dark, sparkling mineral in the center. Zinc is extracted from sphalerite. (Illinois State Museum Collection)

Lead ore occurs in vertical, jointlike fissures, or crevices, in the dolomite bedrock, and as residual deposits at or near the surface of the ground (Figures 5-16 and 3-15). These are commonly referred to as crevice deposits to distinguish them from the deeper deposits of zinc and other types of lead deposits found in the same general area. The latter are termed flat-and-pitch deposits.

Along a typical single crevice, minable concentrations of lead ore are scattered along the trend of the crevice. Pods of lead ore range in length from a few feet to several hundred feet. In many places, pieces of galena have fallen from the walls and have become mixed with the weathered clay and dolomite sand in the open crevices. These crevice deposits occur mainly in the Galena Formation. The flat-and-pitch deposits, on the other hand, occur in the underlying Platteville Formation, also of dolomite (Fig. 5-17). These consist of "flats," which are nearly horizontal, sheetlike bodies of ore, principally zinc, between or parallel to the bedding planes of the strata, and "pitches," which are similar bodies cutting across the bedding planes. The pitches usually slope more than 45 degrees, and many steepen upward to grade into vertical crevices.

Fig. 5-14. Waste piles of crushed rock, called chat, and abandoned mining equipment, are all that remain of a former zinc and lead mine south of Galena, Jo Daviess County.

Two theories have been proposed to explain the origin of these mineral deposits. Hydrothermal solutions, rising from a deeper magmatic source, may have interacted chemically with the dolomite to produce the galena and sphalerite. Many economic mineral deposits around the world are known to have formed in this way. A more detailed explanation of the hydrothermal process is found in Chapter 7.

Although this is a logical explanation, igneous rock of post-Precambrian age, unfortunately, is unknown in the region, even in the subsurface, and no other source for hydrothermal solutions is likely. Both galena and sphalerite are sulfate minerals, and recent studies of their sulfur isotope ratios, as well as analyses of microscopic bubbles trapped during the growth of these ore minerals, have raised additional questions regarding the magmatic origin, the hydrothermal origin, of the ore-depositing solutions

Growing evidence suggests a sedimentary source for the sulfur. As an alternative to the hydrothermal theory, the sedimentary theory proposes that the lead and zinc may have been obtained from the surrounding

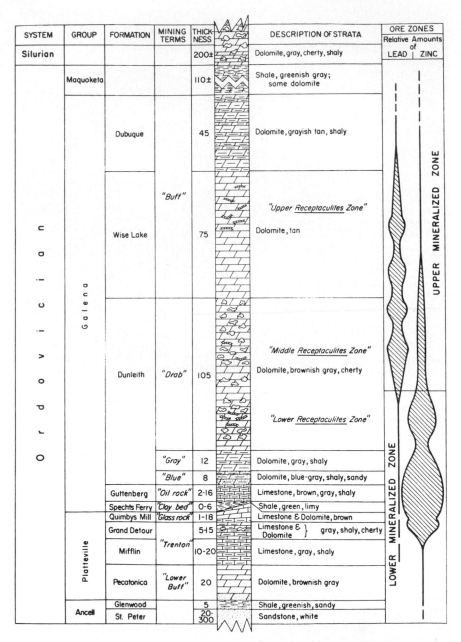

SYSTEM	GROUP	FORMATION	MINING TERMS	THICK-NESS		DESCRIPTION OF STRATA	ORE ZONES Relative Amounts of	
							LEAD	ZINC
Silurian				200±		Dolomite, gray, cherty, shaly		
	Maquoketa			110±		Shale, greenish gray; some dolomite		
Ordovician	Galena	Dubuque		45		Dolomite, grayish tan, shaly		
		Wise Lake	"Buff"	75		"Upper Receptaculites Zone" Dolomite, tan		UPPER MINERALIZED ZONE
		Dunleith	"Drab"	105		"Middle Receptaculites Zone" Dolomite, brownish gray, cherty "Lower Receptaculites Zone"		
	Platteville		"Gray"	12		Dolomite, gray, shaly		LOWER MINERALIZED ZONE
			"Blue"	8		Dolomite, blue-gray, shaly, sandy		
		Guttenberg	"Oil rock"	2-16		Limestone, brown, gray, shaly		
		Spechts Ferry	"Clay bed"	0-6		Shale, green, limy		
		Quimbys Mill	"Glass rock"	1-18		Limestone & Dolomite, brown		
		Grand Detour	"Trenton"	5-15		Limestone & Dolomite } gray, shaly, cherty		
		Mifflin		10-20		Limestone, gray, shaly		
		Pecatonica	"Lower Buff"	20		Dolomite, brownish gray		
	Ancell	Glenwood		5		Shale, greenish, sandy		
		St. Peter		20-300		Sandstone, white		

Fig. 5-15. This stratigraphic column shows the relationship of the lead- and zinc-bearing strata. The relative amounts of each ore are shown on the right. Miners were able to recognize the ore-bearing strata by the presence of *Receptaculites,* an easily identified fossil invertebrate. (Illustration courtesy of Illinois State Geological Survey)

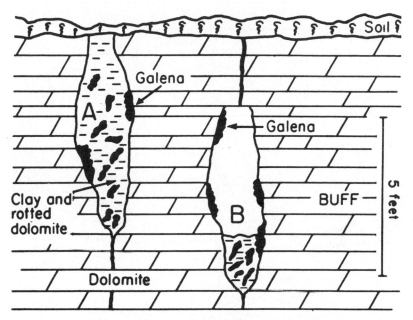

Fig. 5-16. Diagram of a surface crevice mine *(Fig. 3-15)*. (Illustration courtesy of Illinois State Geological Survey)

limestone rocks through a process known as lateral secretion. Lateral secretion is a theory of ore genesis proposed in the eighteenth century that postulates the formation of some ore bodies by the leaching and the removal of the crucial metals from the nearby rock. Subsurface water, moving imperceptibly slow, passes through the surrounding limestone and dolomite, gradually removes and then concentrates the lead and zinc into the presently rich deposits. Prior to lateral secretion, the lead and zinc was widely scattered throughout the surrounding rock as metallic elements and larger but microscopic-sized compounds of lead and zinc sulfide; with lateral secretion having taken place, the metals are sufficiently concentrated as galena and sphalerite to be economically minable.

While technical disagreements among researchers still remain, a general concensus has emerged. It suggests the component elements of the Mississippi Valley lead and zinc ore deposits were derived from the marine sedimentary rocks that contain the ore bodies. The metallic elements were carried upward in solution by saline brines, concentrated, and then deposited as galena and sphalerite. These brines are thought to have been quite hot, between 175 °F to 450 °F, and the remnants of the original sea in which the limestone formed. They are thought to be similar in many ways to the so-called "oilfield brines." In fact, many researchers see a link between

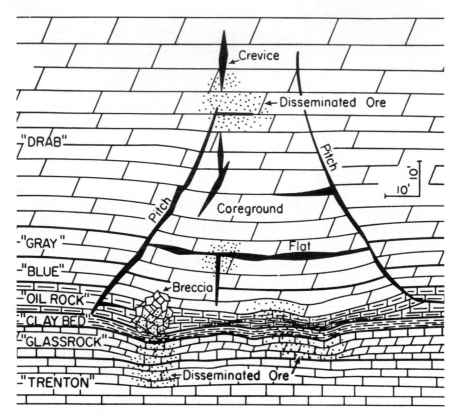

Fig. 5-17. Diagram of an underground flat-and-pitch ore deposit. The rock formations were named by miners. (Courtesy of Illinois State Geological Survey)

the formation of the Mississippi Valley lead and zinc deposits and
petroleum deposits.

Geologists exploring similar mineral deposits are attempting to interpret the histories of past migrations of mineral-rich subsurface waters
through sedimentary rocks of the continental interior, migrations which
occurred hundreds of millions of years ago. Investigations indicate that the
origin of both the shallow lead and zinc deposits in the Galena Dolomite
Formation and the deeper zinc and some lead deposits in the underlying
Platteville Dolomite Formation are similar. Both deposits had a common
origin, either hydrothermal or, more likely, lateral secretion.

The close of the Mississippian Period marked the end of a rather
uniform history of marine sedimentation that began late in the Cambrian
Period. Some of the most fossiliferous sedimentary strata are known from
the Mississippian, the Silurian, and the Ordovician of Illinois. Without
question, the rich lead and zinc ores in the Upper Mississippi Mining
District, the attractive Warsaw-Keokuk geodes, and the ancient sand

beaches preserved in the St. Peter Sandstone Formation are geologic highlights of the early to middle Paleozoic scene. This was a time of geologic tranquillity, a time of wide and warm seas punctuated by occasional muddy and sandy deltas. By the Pennsylvanian all this changed.

Chapter 6
300 Million Years Ago:
Age of the Coal Forests

Whereas the rock strata of the Mississippian Period consist mainly of fossiliferous limestone deposited in comparatively shallow, clear, sunlit, and warm subtropical and tropical seas, the strata of the succeeding Pennsylvanian Period contain little limestone. Instead, almost all the Pennsylvanian-aged strata consist of clastic, or fragmental, rocks. Especially dominant is sandstone, although siltstone and shale also are present. Unlike the thick-bedded Mississippian limestones, the clastic layers of the Pennsylvanian are thin, and they change abruptly from one rock type to another. Coal, too, is a conspicuous rock type although it, together with limestone, makes up less than one percent of the Pennsylvanian strata in Illinois.

Strikingly evident is a repetitive pattern of sandstone followed by shale, then coal, more shale, some limestone, and then a younger shale followed by sandstone again. This relationship is repeated over and over and over throughout the stratigraphic section of about 3,000 vertical feet of Pennsylvanian-aged strata. About 50 distinct coal layers have been recognized and named in Illinois alone, but other coals that are known to be present, still unnamed, bring that total to at least 75. Such a repetitive pattern of rock types is not seen in pre-Pennsylvanian rock systems. Without question, the Pennsylvanian Period represents a special chapter in the physical evolution of Illinois.

Sometime near the end of the Mississippian Period, the shallow and comparatively clear seas that had so consistently covered what today is Illinois became more shallow and murky with mud. Gradual but slow epeirogenic uplift of the continent over the next several hundred thousand years resulted in their eventual withdrawal. The uplifted lands were higher

Facing page. Different rates of erosion between soft and hard Pennsylvanian sandstone layers has resulted in "Old Stone Face" in the Shawnee National Forest near Herod, Pope County. (Photograph courtesy of Illinois State Geological Survey)

to the northeast than in Illinois; so river systems generally flowed into the Illinois region from southeastern Canada. Although a long-term rise of all eastern North America is evident, more localized differential warping occurred on an intermediate scale. Local warping accentuated many above-sea-level land areas. These arches became sources of sediment material that was removed through normal erosional processes, and the intervening basins, often covered by shallow arms of a more distant sea, received the sediment eroded from the upwarps.

Almost all of Illinois, southwestern Indiana, and western Kentucky, were part of the Illinois Basin, a subcircular or spoon-shaped depression, 250 to 300 miles in diameter, described earlier (Figures 5-1 and 1-4). Flanking the northwest-southeast-trending Illinois Basin lay the Ozark Dome to the west, the Cincinnati Arch to the east, and the Nashville Dome to the south. Although these topographic high areas stood near to the basin, they apparently were not the primary source of the sediment that entered the basin. Instead, southeastern Canada seemed to have provided most of the sediment materials that today make up the Pennsylvanian-aged strata in Illinois. Their compositions show a closer affinity to rock types in eastern Canada than to the rock types present in the nearby domes and arches. An ancient river system, the Michigan River, built immense deltas out into the shallow waters of the Illinois Basin in much the same way the modern Mississippi River today is pushing deltas of sediment materials obtained from the midcontinent into the Gulf of Mexico in Louisiana (Fig. 6-1). Ever-so-slight epeirogenic land movements would cause the delta to submerge or emerge as the seas rose and fell and permitted the front to shift for hundreds of miles with each change. This cyclic, or repetitive, oscillation of transgressions and regressions is reflected in the repetitive pattern of the Pennsylvanian rock types. This movement allowed vast coastal swamps containing a lush junglelike vegetation to periodically thrive between times of marine transgressions. The Dismal Swamp in Virginia, the Florida Everglades, and the south Louisiana swamps are modern examples of such lush coastal swamps. Those of the Pennsylvanian age supported a series of forests that were transformed over the millions of years into the 75, or so, distinct coal layers recognized today.

Studies of the coal deposits reveal that many kinds of plants were living at the time, and they contributed their organic matter to the formation of each of the coal layers (Fig. 6-2). Dominating almost all of the other plants in these Pennsylvanian swamps were large, scale-barked trees known commonly as lycopsids. *Lepidodendron* and *Sigillaria* are two of the better-known examples (Figures 6-3 and 6-4). As a tree, *Lepidodendron* tapered gradually, reaching heights of a hundred feet or more, with diameters of up to two feet. The bark of the trunk and branches was characterized by a distinctive, diamond-shaped pattern in which each unit represented the former attachment point of a fallen leaf. *Lepidodendron* means scalelike

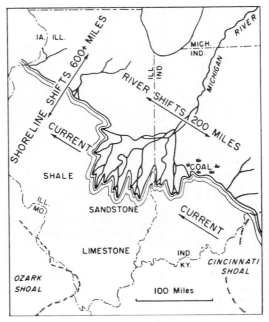

Fig. 6-1. Paleogeographic map of the Illinois-Indiana region during Pennsylvanian time. The Michigan River was building a delta into the shallow sea to the south. While sand, silt, and lime were accumulating in the sea, coastal swamp forests flourished on the adjacent lands. The plant debris that accumulated as thick mats of peat eventually turned into bituminous coal. (Map courtesy of Illinois State Geological Survey)

tree and refers to this visible pattern of leaf scars. Needlelike to lance-shaped leaves, called *Lepidophyllum*, grew as long as two feet on such lycopsid trees as *Lepidodendron* and *Sigillaria*. The roots of lycopod trees are referred to as *Stigmaria* (Figures 6-5 and 6-6). Irregular spirals of circular scars appear on the surfaces of *Stigmaria*, marking the attachment points of the former rootlets. A central pit in each scar indicates the position of the vascular bundle that carried the nutrients from the soil through the rootlet into the tree. Between these rootlet scars pass longitudinal undulating lines or wrinkles. For many years *Stigmaria* was thought to represent the trunk or stem of a distinct type of lycopod tree, the scars marking the attachment places of fallen leaves. But when *Stigmaria* was found clearly associated with the fossil stumps of *Lepidodendron* and *Sigillaria* it was evident that *Stigmaria* was not a distinct tree after all but only the root structure of a lycopod.

These examples of *Stigmaria* and *Lepidophyllum* point out a particular problem unique to paleobotanical studies. When studying living plants, the botanist is able to observe the complete organism and to classify each plant by its scientific name. Only rarely is a plant fossil found complete and intact. Instead, the fossil stems, roots, leaves, and reproductive structures

1. *Lepidodendron*   5. *Calamites*
2. *Sigillaria*   6. *Cordaites*
3. *Neuropteris*   7. *Annularia*
4. *Sphenophyllum*

Fig. 6-2. A Pennsylvanian, coal-forming swamp reconstructed as a living biome. Our valuable coal reserves developed from swamps such as this. (Illustration courtesy of Field Museum of Natural History)

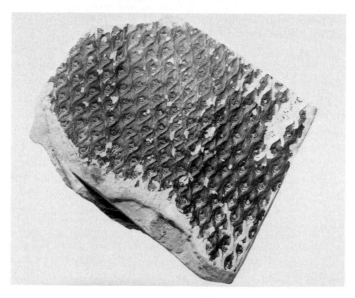

Fig. 6-3. Fossil of *Lepidodendron*. (Illinois State Museum Collection)

Fig. 6-4. Fossil of *Sigillaria*. (Illinois State Museum Collection)

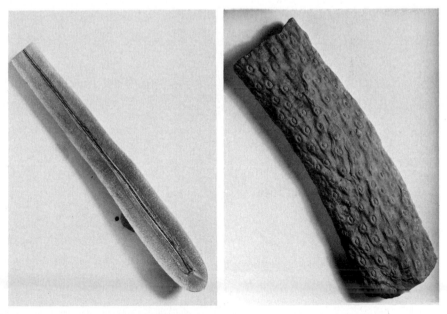

Fig. 6-5. Fossil of *Lepidophyllum (left)*. (Illinois State Museum Collection)

Fig. 6-6. Fossil of *Stigmaria (right)*. (Illinois State Museum Collection)

such as seeds, spores, and fruits invariably are isolated-and detached from each other. Moreover, plant materials begin to decompose almost immediately at the time of death so that often very little remains to be buried. Often it is impossible to piece together the isolated parts and thereby arrive at an accurate reconstruction of the whole plant. Quite commonly, paleobotanists give these various plant parts different names, even though they may belong to the same plant; *Lepidophyllum*, for instance, is the leaf of the *Lepidodendron* tree, and *Stigmaria* is its root structure.

Less common than *Lepidodendron*, but equally widespread, was *Sigillaria*. In contrast to the former, *Sigillaria* seldom bore branches. In this respect it more nearly resembled the modern palm tree (Fig. 6-7). This lycopod attained heights in excess of one hundred feet, with diameters up to six feet. The straight, gently tapering trunk was surmounted by a cluster of long, grasslike leaves. After the leaves had dropped from the trees, a series of leaf scars, usually hexagonal in general outline, became visible on the bark. The scars occurred directly above one another in vertical columns, and each column is separated by a straight furrow extending the full length of the trunk.

Fig. 6-7. Restoration of a *Sigillaria* tree. The tall, unbranched trunk was usually topped by a crown of long, narrow leaves. (Illustration courtesy of Field Museum of Natural History)

In addition to the various forms of lycopod trees, the coal forests contained a variety of other tall trees, especially *Cordaites* (Fig. 6-8). Also attaining heights in excess of one hundred feet, *Cordaites* bore three-foot-long straplike leaves in a spiral arrangement around its branches. The leaves are termed *Cordaites* and the trunks—which are exceedingly rare—are termed *Cordaicladus.*

Fig. 6-8. Fossil of *Cordaites.* (Illinois State Museum Collection)

Gigantic rushlike plants also flourished in the Pennsylvanian swamps. *Calamites* is a distant relative of the modern low-growing *Equisetum*, commonly called horsetail, scouring-rush, or jointed grass, that today grows in wet areas. Fossil casts of *Calamites* may measure a foot or more in diameter (Fig. 6-9). The leaves were borne in whorls completely surrounding the branches. Called either *Annularia* or *Asterophyllites*, leaves of *Calamites* resemble asters and so have been commonly called "fossil asters" (Fig. 6-10). The leaves of *Calamites*, spread out in a single plane, may be linear, lanceolate, or spatulate. *Annularia* are united at the base to form a small collar around the stem.

Fig. 6-9. Fossil of *Calamites.* (Illinois State Museum Collection)

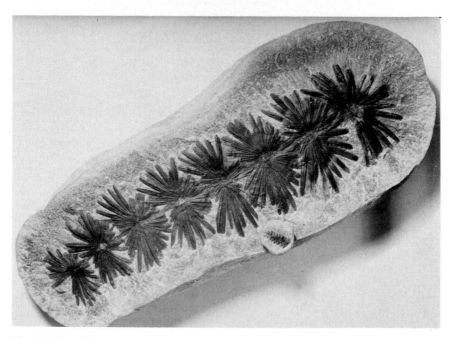

Fig. 6-10. Fossil of *Annularia.* (Illinois State Museum Collection)

All the plants living at this time were not of the immense proportions of the lycopods and *Cordaites*. A varied undergrowth of much smaller and more delicate plants flourished beneath these giants, much like the small plants that thrive in the underbrush of modern forests. During Pennsylvanian time, these smaller plants included *Sphenophyllum*, *Neuropteris*, *Alethopeteris*, and *Pecopteris* (Fig. 6-11).

Fig. 6-11. Fossil of *Sphenophyllum*. (Illinois State Museum Collection)

Many of the fossil plants are preserved as black or dark gray carbonaceous impressions (Fig. 6-12). Unlike the colorful petrified wood of northern Arizona in which every minute, detailed structure of the plant has been precisely replaced by colorful quartz minerals such as jasper and chalcedony, the fossil plants of the Illinois Basin remain only as imprints of a dark carbon film. Such a thin layer of carbon forms when organic matter slowly decomposes under water or sediment and gradually loses its organic content. In the absence of oxygen, normal decay cannot take place. The oxygen, hydrogen, and nitrogen originally present in the organic compounds of the plant are decreased to the extent that only a thin film of carbon-rich material remains. This carbon residue often retains the form and identifiable characteristics of the original plant structure. Fossils having undergone this kind of preservation are often referred to as compressions because of the compressive forces required to bring about the concentration of carbon. Compression fossils are formed by a process known as carbonization in which the original carbon of the plant has been concentrated.

Fig. 6-12. Carbonaceous imprint of *Megalopteris,* a plant that grew mainly on the drier uplands adjacent to the swamp forests during Pennsylvanian time. (Illinois State Museum Collection)

The abundant plant fossils in coal beds clearly indicate that they originated in freshwater swamps, much as peat bogs today form under freshwater conditions. As the luxuriant plant growth of such a swamp dies, it falls onto the water-logged soil. The water, and rapid burial by the quick addition of falling leaves, protect the twigs, branches, leaves, fruits, and seeds from oxidizing further, or decaying.

As plant material continues to accumulate, it gradually turns to peat, a porous brown mass of organic matter in which twigs, roots, and other plant parts can still be recognized. With further chemical transformations of the aging organic matter, the carbon becomes more concentrated and the peat turns into lignite, a very soft coallike material. Greater depth of burial, still more time, and higher temperature may further change the lignite to bituminous, or soft coal. During this step, the gaseous, or volatile elements of oxygen, hydrogen, and nitrogen of the original plant are almost completely driven off, thereby concentrating the original carbon of the plant. Bituminous coal contains not less than 85 percent carbon while anthracite, or hard coal, the end product of the coal-forming process, contains not less than 95 percent carbon.

In both bituminous and anthracite, none of the original plant structures are recognized. The typical ratio of thicknesses of uncompacted peat transformed to coal is about ten to one. To develop a sizable amount of commercial grade coal several feet thick requires an enormous quantity of vegetation—especially since most of it probably decayed completely before the plant materials had the chance to enter the coal-forming cycle. During this time, the climate is assumed to have been not only warm but also quite humid. The trees lacked growth rings and had large, thin-walled cells in their trunks suggesting no distinct seasonal changes in temperature and humidity, thus allowing a rapid growth rate. Fossils of amphibians and reptiles found along with the plant fossils support the reconstruction of a tropical environment. Amphibians and reptiles do not tolerate pronounced changes in temperature.

During the Pennsylvanian Period, Illinois probably lay along the equator, or a few degrees south of it. With the opening of the Atlantic Ocean, 120 million years later, Illinois moved slowly away from this equatorial position and drifted northward and westward to its present latitude.

It was pointed out earlier in this chapter that the Pennsylvanian strata, about 3,000 feet thick, reveal a repetitive pattern of certain rock types. Included are about 75 distinct coal layers. The repetition of about five or six distinct rock layers is called a cyclothem (Fig. 6-13). Cyclothems vary greatly in thickness and lateral extent; they usually are not much more than about 30 feet thick, often much less. A single, complete cyclothem is rare; it is thought that the cyclothem begins ideally with the buildup of a massive and relatively thick-bedded sandstone resting on older strata. This sandstone appears to have been formed by river processes rather than having been laid down on a sea floor. Overlying this terrestrial, or nonmarine, sandstone is usually a gray sandy shale over which, in turn, lies a distinctively light, almost bleached-looking, gray shale that often contains abundant casts of *Stigmaria*. This light-gray shale is identified as the underclay. Resting directly on the underclay is the several-foot-thick coal bed.

The lower half of the cyclothem, that is, from the sandstone to the top of the coal bed, is interpreted as having formed in the following manner. The influx of sand, which later became the sandstone, marked the beginning of the formation of a delta into a shallow sea. It indicates the onset of nonmarine or freshwater conditions. The massive, basal sandstone grades laterally into horizontal shaly and finer-grained sandstones that were deposited farther and farther out in the shallow sea. Marshy conditions, with brackish water at first, began to develop on the delta lowland. As the water became less saline with the sea regressing farther offshore, a freshwater swamp followed the brackish-water marsh. In its shallow and quiet water, only the finest clays were deposited. These fine clays are identified today as the underclay. As the clay accumulated, a dense forest spread over the newly emerged land of the delta, and a long interval of several tens of thousands of years of peat accumulation began. The underclay is thought to be the soil horizon into which the roots of *Lepidodendron*, *Sigillaria*, *Cordaites* and others of these giant trees were anchored.

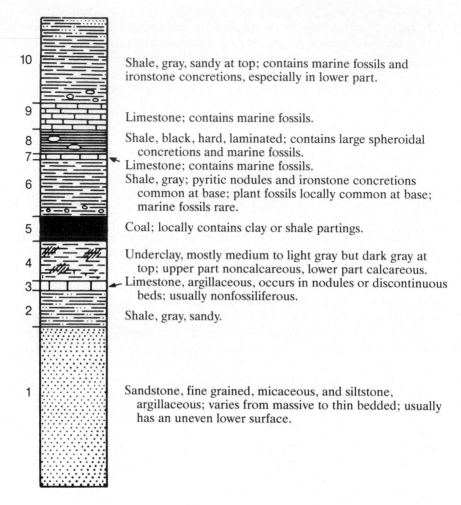

10 Shale, gray, sandy at top; contains marine fossils and ironstone concretions, especially in lower part.

9 Limestone; contains marine fossils.

8 Shale, black, hard, laminated; contains large spheroidal concretions and marine fossils.

7 Limestone; contains marine fossils.

6 Shale, gray; pyritic nodules and ironstone concretions common at base; plant fossils locally common at base; marine fossils rare.

5 Coal; locally contains clay or shale partings.

4 Underclay, mostly medium to light gray but dark gray at top; upper part noncalcareous, lower part calcareous.

3 Limestone, argillaceous, occurs in nodules or discontinuous beds; usually nonfossiliferous.

2 Shale, gray, sandy.

1 Sandstone, fine grained, micaceous, and siltstone, argillaceous; varies from massive to thin bedded; usually has an uneven lower surface.

Fig. 6-13. Cross section of a complete cyclothem. When developed under ideal conditions, it consists of ten sedimentary layers. About 50 cyclothems have been described in the Illinois Basin, but others may occur. Only a few cyclothems contain all ten layers. Conditions under which the sediments accumulated varied widely and resulted in the absence of individual layers in different cyclothems. Units 1 through 5 are nonmarine and were deposited on the coastal lowlands from which the sea had withdrawn. Units 6 through 10 are marine sediments and were deposited when the sea readvanced over the delta lowland. The underclay (4), coal (5), black shale (8), and limestone (9) of an individual cyclothem, although usually only a few feet thick, can be widely distributed. Some individual coal seams, traced in outcrops and mines and identified in subsurface drill records, are found in several states. The concept of the cyclothem developed out of field studies originally conducted in western Illinois in the early 1930s. (Illustration courtesy of Illinois State Geological Survey)

In a single cyclothem, the transition from the nonmarine condition just described to a marine condition is abrupt. The land appears to have subsided quickly and the sea advanced over the swamp. As the waters became increasingly salty from the encroaching sea, the forest was killed and peat deposition ceased. For a time, the shallow water was brackish and foul. The dark gray and black organic mud—now the black shale that overlies the coal bed—continued to accumulate, burying in ever-thickening layers of black mud the peat and other organic remains of the former junglelike forest. The weight of these sediments initiated the transformation of peat into lignite and then, as more time elapsed, the change of lignite to bituminous coal. These same black shales often contain the fossilized remains of marine-dwelling invertebrates; these indicate the presence of open marine conditions.

As the sea advanced farther inland and gradually deepened, the warm, tropical water cleared, and purer limestone began to be deposited. Some mud, however, continued to accumulate during this time of limestone deposition. Evidence for these events is the shaly character of the limestone. Overlying the limestone is a younger shale, and its presence signals the interruption of limestone deposition as the hitherto retreating delta front began to build seaward again. The rapid influx of such mud over the limestone marked the end of the cycle and the start of the succeeding cyclothem. As the delta front continued to build seaward, massive river-sand deposition began again and marked the onset of the next cycle of sedimentation, the beginning of the second cyclothem.

Just what caused this constant repetition of one cyclothem after another during the Pennsylvanian, with the combined weight of all the sediments exerting sufficient pressure to convert the peat and lignite into bituminous coal? Many theories have been suggested. The most plausible suggests that worldwide fluctuations of sea levels were due perhaps to periodic advances and retreats of continental glaciers known to have developed on the southern hemisphere continents at this time. Additional large-scale warpings of the deep-sea floor itself may have reinforced these sea level changes. Perhaps repetitive fluctuations in the amount of clastic sediments supplied to the deltas, possibly in response to cyclic climatic changes affecting the amount of erosion in the uplands, may have been another reason. As more sediment was supplied, deltas advance; transgression occurred when sediment supply decreased. Large-scale epeirogenic land movements, associated with continental drift and plate tectonics, no doubt also played a significant role. The answer to the question is not an easy one. But one statement can be expressed with certainty: the physical history of the North American continent during the Pennsylvanian Period, particularly in Illinois and the Midwest, provided a suitable physical environment to produce one of the richest of our energy resources—coal (Fig. 6-14).

Fig. 6-14. Coal about 1,000 feet underground is mined in Hamilton County. The 8-foot-thick coal seam has been removed and miners are securing the overlying "roof" rock. (Photograph courtesy of Illinois Coal Association, Springfield, Illinois)

Rocks bearing coal underlie about 13 percent of the United States. Coal is present in at least 36 states and is mined in 25, of which Illinois is the fifth largest producer after Kentucky, West Virginia, Wyoming, and Pennsylvania. Coal represents about 82 percent of America's known recoverable energy resources. In comparison, petroleum and natural gas together amount to only a little more than six percent.

In Illinois, coal-bearing Pennsylvanian strata underlie about 65 percent of the land area, including all or parts of at least 86 of the 102 counties in the state. An estimated 181 billion tons of coal still remain in the ground in Illinois. This total includes all coal beds over 28 inches thick that can be economically mined by underground methods and those as thin as 18 inches but less than 150 feet deep, that can, therefore, be economically mined from the surface. Only 30 billion of the 181 billion tons, however, are recoverable—coal that can be legally, economically, and technically mined using present-day methods. This means that Illinois has almost one-eighth of the total recoverable reserves of all types of coal in the United States, that is, anthracite, bituminous, and lesser ranks classified by degree of hardness, moisture, and energy content. On the other hand, Illinois contains about 25 percent of the nation's total recoverable bituminous coal reserves, an impressive figure to say the least. Bituminous is soft coal, the type most often used in the United States to generate electricty and to make coke for the steel industry.

Five billion tons of coal have been mined in Illinois since about 1810, when commercial mining is reported to have first started in Jackson County, through 1984 when over 65 million tons were produced. In 1984, Kentucky produced just over 164 million tons, and Texas, the sixth-ranking producer, slightly over 41 million tons. About 20 coal seams have been mined in Illinois on and off through the years, each specifically named and numbered. About 50 coals are named and numbered, such as the Harrisburg (No. 5) Coal, the Briar Hill (No. 5A) Coal, and the Herrin (No. 6) Coal. The numbers were assigned by early geologists in the middle 1800s when they discovered that the coals not only were widespread but could be arranged in an orderly stratigraphic sequence, one above the other. They consecutively numbered the coal beds from the oldest, or the lowest, to the youngest, or the highest in the sequence. Later, however, it was discovered that additional coal beds not previously recognized needed to be included, thereby complicating the numbering system. Letter designations, such as No. 5A, were added for a while, but it was finally decided to used geographic names for the coal beds in accordance with the standard practice of stratigraphic nomenclature. Because of established usage, however, the numbers are still used along with the geographic names for the more widespread and commercially important coal seams.

The overwhelming bulk of Illinois coal production, nearly 90 percent, in fact, has come from the Herrin (No. 6) and the underlying Springfield (No. 5) seams. Herrin coal, the most extensively mined in Illinois, constitutes about 42 percent of the state's total coal resources. It is the chief source of coal in southwestern and southern Illinois where the largest number of mines operate. The No. 6 coal has its greatest thickness and lowest ash and sulfur content, in the area of Franklin, Williamson, and Jefferson counties. Both ash and sulfur are natural ingredients in coal that, unfortunately, produce unwanted contaminants when the coal is burned and which somehow must be removed. The Herrin coal is up to 14 feet thick in places, an unusual thickness since the average thickness in active mines in the region is about eight feet. The No. 5 coal has been extensively tapped in western Illinois and in the Springfield and Harrisburg vicinities where it has a common thickness of four to six feet.

Although the geology and the fossilized remains of the Pennsylvanian coal swamps have been intensively studied, a variety of other, unfamiliar plants are known to have also lived on the nearby higher and drier lands. These so-called "upland flora" flourished at the same time as those in the wet, low, coal-forming swamps, but not much is known about them because their fossilized remains are quite rare. Plants and animals living in swamps are more likely to be preserved than those living in the drier, harsher, less-protected, above-water environments. Therefore, disproportionately more is known about the kind of life that flourished in the coal swamps than in those environments elsewhere in which fossilized remains are relatively scarce.

Several Pennsylvanian rock exposures containing a record of upland flora have been found near Mt. Sterling in Brown County and at Milan in Rock Island County in western Illinois. These are two of the several localities known to exist worldwide in which such Pennsylvanian upland flora occur. Fossils contained in these strata have allowed reconstructions to be made for the drier and higher "Coal Age" uplands. These, not surprisingly, reveal a plant assemblage different from that of the wetter lowlands.

Whereas the swamp flora is dominated by such lycopods as *Lepidodendron*, *Sigillaria*, and *Calamites*, the seed ferns seem to dominate the upland flora. Even among the seed ferns, the types represented are not the same as those seen in the swamp floras. One rock exposure studied in Brown County reveals a distinctive upland flora that flourished near a 40-foot-deep ravine eroded into older Mississippian limestone during early Pennsylvanian time. The ravine narrows from 40 feet at the top to 15 feet at the bottom and is filled with mud, silt, and sand—now in the form of fissile shale and sandstone beds—of Pennsylvanian age (Fig. 6-15). Sand and plant parts from the higher lands nearby were washed into the deepening ravine by storms and seasonal rains. Similar channels, shallower and narrower with nearly vertical side walls, are seen in still older Devonian strata exposed in several limestone quarries in Rock Island County; they, too, are filled with fossil-bearing shales and sandstones.

The early Pennsylvanian shale and sandstone sediments filling these channels, which were eroded into the older Mississippian or Devonian limestones, contain the fossil remains of nearly 30 types of upland plants. Several of these are not represented on the coal-forming swamps. Other plants, common in the swamps, are absent in these upland areas. Among the plants unique to the early Pennsylvanian uplands are *Megalopteris*, *Lesleya*, *Lacoea*, and *Palaeopteridium*.

Megalopteris and *Lesleya* (Fig. 6-12), in particular, grew well on the comparatively dry soils derived from the disintegrating and decomposing underlying limestone bedrock. They can be seen in Figure 6-16 growing on the low hill almost to the exclusion of other plants at what is today Milan in Rock Island County. With their long, pointed leaves—some single-lobed, some three-lobed—they were unlike anything now living. Tall *Lepidodendron* and *Calamites* trees crowded the shoreline of a shallow bay connected with a larger sea. Bushes of *Cordaites* and seed ferns grew a short distance from the shore. *Megalopteris* and *Lesleya* grew on the higher and drier ground farther from the shore, on the 15-foot-high hill that faced the bay. In all probablity, both *Megalopteris* and *Lesleya* were large trees. Some of

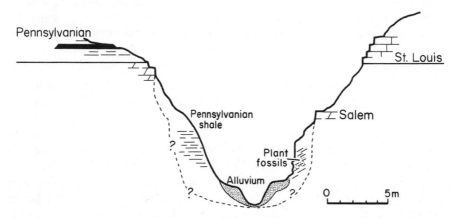

Fig. 6-15. This cross section shows a ravine eroded into Mississippian limestone during Pennsylvanian time. (Illustration courtesy of R. Leary, Illinois State Museum)

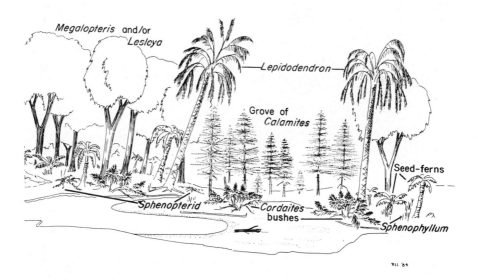

Fig. 6-16. Reconstruction of a small bay during Pennsylvanian time in western Illinois as it might have appeared before a rising sea level covered the small islands. *Lepidodendron, Calamites, Cordaites,* and the small *Sphenophyllum* and *Sphenopterid* are growing in the low-lying wet areas. *Megalopteris* and *Lesleya* are growing on the higher and drier lands, an elevation difference of about 20 feet. (Illustration courtesy of R. Leary, Illinois State Museum)

the plants were blown from the hilltop; others fell and were washed into the three-foot-deep embayment. In due course, they were buried by mud and silt slowly accumulating there. However, fossils of these drier upland floras are not abundant, and to accurately reconstruct them is a matter of some speculation.

A single specimen of a fossil scorpion was found in the same limestone quarry containing fossils of the upland flora at Milan (Fig. 6-17). Scorpions are ancient organisms; fully developed individuals are found in rock strata of late Silurian age in both New York State and Sweden. Other, younger specimens are known from Pennsylvanian deposits at Mazon Creek in northern Illinois. *Labriscorpio alliedensis*, as the one from Milan has been named, is of possible late Mississippian or very early Pennsylvanian age, and its discovery fills a gap between those known from the late Silurian Period and those clearly of the Pennsylvanian Period.

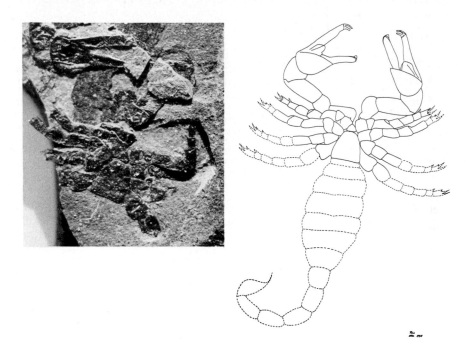

Fig. 6-17. A fossil scorpion, *Labriscorpio alliedensis,* as found in a quarry in western Illinois *(left)*. In the reconstruction of the fossil animal *(right)*, solid lines outline the fossilized material, and dashed lines depict the probable appearance of the rest of the scorpion. (Drawing courtesy of R. Leary, Illinois State Museum)

No discussion of the Pennsylvanian Period of Illinois, no matter how brief, would be complete without reference to the fossil-rich concretions that abound at Mazon Creek in Grundy and Will counties. Although concretions are not an unusual feature of sedimentary rocks, the fossils contained within those at Mazon Creek are unique. The fossils occur in spheroidal and elliptical concretions that range in size from about one-quarter inch to 12 inches in length (Fig. 6-18). Concretions are hard, compact masses of mineral matter formed by orderly and highly localized deposition in water around a central nucleus at the same time the rest of the sediments were accumulating. In this case, the mineral matter was siderite, an iron carbonate mineral, forming around a nucleus of fossil matter. Although the origin of concretions is poorly understood, somehow the cementing siderite tended to concentrate around a common centerpoint when entering the unconsolidated sediment. For reasons that are unclear, the siderite is more firmly bound together than are the particles of the host rock that surround the concretion. As a result, concretions characteristically display distinct boundaries and can easily be separated from the rest of the rock.

The siderite, or ironstone concretions as they sometimes are called, occur in the Francis Creek Shale and are famous for their rich fossil fauna and flora. A single blow of the hammer can split open a concretion and reveal the fossil preserved within. Over 350 kinds of plants and more than 320 kinds of animals have been described, many known only from this location. Also seen in many of the concretions is a fine preservation of the soft anatomy of animals. That is rare, indeed. Those at Mazon Creek contain numerous examples of soft tentacles of jellyfish, hatchling fish with yolk sac attached, and the eggs of other creatures. On some clams, insects, and fish, even the pattern of coloration is preserved. Similar fossil-bearing concretions are known from Carterville near Carbondale, in Jackson County, and from Terre Haute, Indiana.

Two processes were responsible for the unusual degree of preservation: rapid burial prevented decomposition, and formation of the ironstone concretion itself protected the organism. The Mazon Creek flora and fauna thus present a record of soft-bodied animals as well as those with hard skeletal parts almost unequalled anywhere. A comprehensive record of the vegetation growing at that time is also well preserved. From what can be determined, it seems that the plants and animals lived on a delta where one or more large, sluggish rivers from the north entered a shallow subtropical sea then occupying the Illinois Basin and covering most of Illinois. Two diverse habitats seem to be represented: the swampy, forested lowland of the delta and the shallow coastal waters just beyond the delta.

In the litter of the forest floor lived millipedes, centipedes, scorpions, spiders, and various amphibians that preyed on them. Freshwater fishes, shrimps, horseshoe crabs, and other small aquatic forms inhabited the

Fig. 6-18. A Mazon Creek concretion opened to reveal the fossilized frond of *Odon-topteris,* a treelike fern. (Illinois State Museum Collection)

ponds, bayous, and channels that drained through the forest and out across the delta.

In the second habitat of the warm, near-shore waters of the delta lived a diverse fauna including coelenterates (coral and soft-bodied jellyfishlike animals), worms, molluscs, sea cucumberlike animals, shrimps, and fishes. Throughout the years, the mining of the coal has progressed continuously over a wider and wider area and, as a result, has uncovered an almost endless supply of new concretions. Thousands of collectors from near and far have been attracted to Mazon Creek to comb the pits in quest of these prized finds. Their activities have brought to light many finely preserved specimens, and their study has added measurably to a better understanding of the Pennsylvanian Period. Today, unfortunately, collecting is both limited and prohibited. Much of the land has been reclaimed by coal companies, active pits require prior permission to enter, and areas still available to collectors have been thoroughly picked over, leaving poor prospect of finding specimens of interest or value.

The Pennsylvanian Period ended about 270 million years ago, concluding an interesting chapter in the geologic development of Illinois. This was a time of the giant forests and the fascinating Mazon Creek concretions. Conditions, too, were suitable for the formation of coal, an energy resource of immense value today. Sedimentary rocks from the succeeding Permian, Triassic, and Jurassic periods are not present in Illinois. Whether they were never deposited or if they had been deposited and were then subsequently removed by erosion is difficult to say. About 170 million years of geologic history is missing in Illinois from this time interval. Not until the Cretaceous Period, about 100 million years ago, is a rock record found preserved in Illinois and the geologic trail again resumed.

Chapter 7
100 Million Years Ago:
Fluorite, the State Mineral of Illinois, is Formed

One of the better-known chapters in Earth's history is the Mesozoic Era, an interval that began about 230 million years ago and ended about 65 million years ago. The Mesozoic follows the earlier Paleozoic Era and preceded the subsequent Cenozoic Era. It is popularly known as the Age of Reptiles. Although reptilian ancestry dates back to the late Paleozoic, the Mesozoic was the domain of such familiar giants as the dinosaurs on land; the ichthyosaurs, plesiosaurs, and mosasaurs in the seas; and the pterosaurs in the air. It was a time of saurian dominance, large and small. Saurian is a term derived from the Latin meaning reptile.

Unfortunately for Illinoians, rock strata of this vintage are not found in abundance in this state. Only a few strata of Cretaceous age, that is, the last period of Mesozoic time, are found in southern Illinois—in Alexander, Pulaski, and Massac counties—and in western Illinois north and southeast of Quincy in Adams and Pike counties. Cretaceous-aged strata in southern Illinois are as much as 500 feet thick near Cairo but thin rapidly toward the north. Evidently, these sediments were laid down in a large delta built by a river flowing from the east into a broad arm of the sea known today as the Mississippi Embayment. In western Illinois, the strata are much thinner, only about 100 feet thick, and are detached remnants of extensive Cretaceous sediments that at one time covered the entire region east of the Rocky Mountains and north of the Missouri Ozarks. All these Cretaceous strata are termed the Gulfian Series. In western Illinois, they appear to be beach and nearshore sediments that were deposited in an advancing sea some 70 or 80 million years ago.

Facing page. Fluorite ore stockpiled for processing at the Ozark-Mahoning Mine in Rosiclare, Hardin County. The fluorite mining district in southern Illinois accounts for 90 percent of production in the United States. (Photograph courtesy of M. Schnorf, State of Illinois, Office of Comptroller)

Conceivably, the Cretaceous strata in Illinois could contain the fossiliz-ed remains of marine reptiles, such as plesiosaurs, ichthyosaurs, mosasaurs, or of the trachodont, a coastal, swamp-dwelling dinosaur. But not a trace of such fossils has been uncovered to date. Instead, abundant fossils of tiny, one-celled marine invertebrates, called foraminifera, are found in con-siderable numbers. Abundant plant remains also are found in some of the lignitic beds. Perhaps dinosaur fossils may yet be found in the Cretaceous strata of Illinois; dinosaur bone fragments recently have been discovered in the Cretaceous of Iowa. Illinois paleontologists hope that such might be the case, and so their search continues.

Sometime during the 165 million years of the Mesozoic Era, a material of almost equal interest as the dinosaurs developed in Illinois, not a fossil but a mineral. Fluorite is its preferred name, although many people call it fluorspar. In the United States, extensive deposits occur in southern Illinois and adjoining Kentucky, the richest concentration of fluorite in North America. Fluorite is a mineral of exquisite beauty, color, symmetry, and perfection of form, a naturally occurring simple compound of two elements, calcium and fluorine (Frontispiece). Its name is derived from the Latin *fluere* which means "to flow." Fluorite melts and flows easily under heat and is essential as a flux in the smelting of many metallic ores.

As a mineral, fluorite is appealing for many reasons. When found in its natural crystal form, fluorite occurs as a simple cube. Although easily broken, it does not split randomly, but instead separates into pyramid-shaped octahedrons, or two four-sided pyramids joined at their bases. Its size is also noteworthy. Crystal clusters of fluorite cubes can be found in almost any size and may weigh as much as several hundred pounds. Usual-ly, crystal groups range from several inches to 20 or 30 feet across; such large sizes are often found in areas undergoing active mining. The most common color is a rich, royal purple, although fluorite frequently occurs in transluscent honey, amber, green, or yellow. Even colorless fluorite is com-mon. Often it is vari-colored, showing zones of color parallel to the crystal cube or octahedron faces. Crystals of fluorite from southern Illinois are equal in beauty to any in the world, although they often do not exhibit the exquisite perfection of Swiss specimens nor the brilliance of English clusters.

Fluorite's physical and chemical properties make it industrially and strategically important, ranking second only to uranium. Uses for this mineral are almost endless: as a flux in steelmaking; as an ingredient of hydrofluoric acid, which in turn is used in the manufacture of aerosols, refrigerants, and teflon; as an oxidizer for rocket fuels; as an insecticide in-gredient; as a deterrent to decay of teeth; in the manufacture of glass, especially for lamp bulbs and "Tiffany" shades and other colored glass; in enamels and glazes; and in such miscellaneous uses as in the manufacture of dental cements and optical lenses. Richly colored fluorite is used as a gemstone in jewelry; native Americans living in the Midwest over a thousand years ago also found fluorite attractive and from it carved figurines and other objects (Fig. 7-1). But its decorative use, unfortunately, is severely limited. Its extreme softness and pronounced cleavage allows flat or sharply angular pieces to constantly shear off even under the slightest impact.

Fig. 7-1. This delicate, fluorite figurine was found at the Angel Site, near Evansville, Indiana. The 10-inch-tall sculpture is a beautiful example of aboriginal craftmanship about 800 to 900 years ago. The fluorite came from southern Illinois or adjacent Kentucky. (Photograph courtesy of Glenn A. Black Laboratory of Archaeology, Indiana University)

Another attractive property of fluorite is its fluorescence, although all fluorite is not fluorescent. Fluorescence refers to the optical property of a material that changes color when taken out of ordinary light and placed under ultraviolet or "black" light.The term is derived from fluorite, one of the first minerals studied that impressively displayed this optical property. Therefore, because of its abundance in southern Illinois, its beauty, its commercial value, and its unusual properties, the 74th Illinois General Assembly in 1965 designated fluorite the state mineral. It joined the ranks of the cardinal, oak, and native violet as state symbols. Since then, the monarch butterfly and white-tailed deer were added as state insect and mammal.

The largest concentration of fluorite in North America—and worldwide for that matter—occurs in southern Illinois and adjoining Kentucky. This mining district, spanning over 700 square miles, was once one of the most productive fluorite districts in the world. In 1983, Illinois produced an estimated 61,000 tons of fluorite, a marked decrease from the 115,000 tons produced in 1981 and 77,000 tons in 1982. Even today, with tonnage reduced from former years, Illinois supplies more than 90 percent of the total fluorite mined in the United States. The balance of domestically produced fluorite is obtained from the five western states of Arizona, Montana, Nevada, Texas, and Utah. Rosiclare, Cave-In-Rock, and Elizabethtown in Hardin and Pope counties are, or have been, the principle headquarter towns for Illinois fluorite. Current production comes almost exclusively from the Cave-In-Rock district. Associated with Illinois fluorite are three other minerals: galena, sphalerite, and barite. Each is a sulfur-bearing mineral of lead, zinc, and barium, respectively. Each, too, is a valuable ore mineral, and minor amounts of lead and zinc are produced in the district. Silver is another metal recovered from the mined fluorite ore. The presence of lead, zinc, barium, and silver add to the overall value of the ore deposit.

In 1983, the latest year for which statistics are available, only 10 percent of the fluorite consumed in the United States was mined in Illinois. Ninety percent was imported from such countries as Mexico, South Africa, Spain, Italy, and Morocco. Why is so much fluorite exported into the United States from these five countries when fluorite reserves are so rich in southern Illinois? Lower price of the imports, especially those originating in Mexico, is the main reason. And China now also is exporting to the United States more of this strategic mineral at equally low prices. Although Illinois production increased about 23 percent in 1981, production decreased 31 percent in 1982. In 1983, fluorite production decreased another 20 percent. The recent recession in the United States steel industry, an important user of fluorite, was a major factor for this latest decline. For these reasons, Illinois's fluorite industry is currently experiencing reduced production and considerable economic hardship.

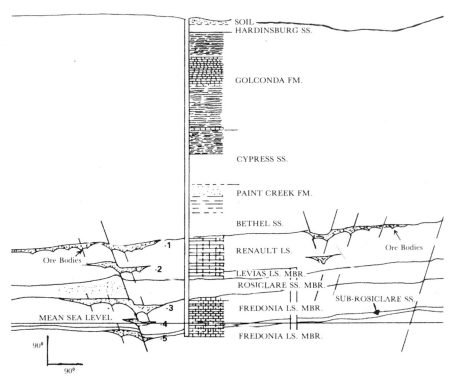

Fig. 7-2. This cross section through the Cave-In-Rock fluorite district shows various horizons of ore with minor faulting. Mineralization of zones 2 through 5 took place within the Ste. Genevieve Limestone; the uppermost zone formed at the top of the Renault Limestone. Both limestones are of Mississippian age. (Illustration courtesy of Illinois State Geological Survey)

The fluorite mineral assemblage occurs in two relatively simple geologic settings: as a bedded deposit or as a vein deposit (Figures 7-2 and 7-3). The bedded deposit is a flat-lying, irregularly shaped body of ore that lies parallel to the sedimentary strata in which it occurs. Ore concentration can range from 200 to more than 10,000 feet in length and from 50 to 300 feet in width. However, these bedded ore bodies are quite thin, usually no more than 15 feet thick. Vein deposits, on the other hand, are steeply inclined, nearly vertical, sheetlike masses of fluorite that occur as fillings in previously opened rock tissues developed along faults. The width and continuity of the vein deposit varies considerably and depends on the width of the original fracture opening. Whether a bedded or a vein deposit, the fluorite is found principally in limestones of Mississippian age. In the bedded deposits, a sandstone layer caps the fluorite-bearing limestone.

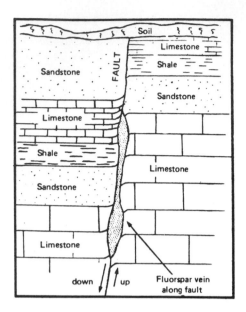

Fig. 7-3. Numerous faults interrupt the bedrock of southern Illinois. Fluorite is concentrated along such faults and is economically minable. A vein deposit is illustrated in this cross section. (Illustration courtesy of Illinois State Geological Survey)

Exactly when the fluorite mineral assemblage originated is difficult to say. As pointed out, the fluorite and associated minerals rarely occur in strata other than those of Mississippian age. It also is known that fluorite did not form at the same time the limestone was deposited. Unlike limestone, which contains calcium carbonate that precipitated from warm, tropical seas, fluorite cannot precipitate from normal sea water. Furthermore, fluorite has not been found in strata of Cenozoic age. Therefore, it must have formed sometime after the Mississippian and before the Cenozoic. Many geologists think that it formed sometime during the Mesozoic but are uncertain if it was early, middle, or late Mesozoic. Perhaps it formed sometime during the Cretaceous. A general figure considered reasonable under the questionable circumstances is about 100 million years ago, or about the middle of Mesozoic time.

How the fluorite assemblage formed requires a more lengthy and complex answer. Geologists have long known that most economically valuable ore deposits, and perhaps those of the fluorite mining district also, result from or relate to some kind of igneous activity. Volcanoes such as Mount St. Helens, Mount Rainier, Mount Hood, and others of the Cascade Range in the Pacific Northwest, for instance, or those of the Hawaiian Islands, are merely the surface manifestations of subterranean, mobile masses of magma. Magma forms and moves about deep underground in response to high heat and pressure, especially in association with the forces involved with the plate tectonic processes. When it reaches the surface it is called lava.

Magmas and lavas are complex solutions of dissolved chemicals that become distinct and identifiable minerals upon solidification. The more common of these minerals are quartz, hornblende, augite, and olivine, and several types of feldspar and mica as discussed in Chapter 2. Appropriately enough, they are called the rock-forming minerals and make up as much as 95 percent of the mineral content of igneous rocks.

What is important to emphasize here, however, is that a magma not only contains the essential chemical ingredients to form the ordinary minerals just described, but it often contains a large quantity of other materials. These include fluids and gases such as water, carbon dioxide, hydrogen sulfide, hydrogen fluoride, and such elements as fluorine, chlorine, nitrogen, and boron. Metallic elements like lead, zinc, barium, iron, germanium, gold, silver, cesium, and other valuable metals may also be present within the magma.

Within all magmas, then, are almost all the chemical elements necessary to form either the ordinary minerals or the much-rarer and economically more-valuable minerals. Unfortunately, the natural chemical ingredients that make up the rarer minerals are widely disseminated throughout a magma so that certain, specific geologic processes are required to sufficiently concentrate and collect them into enriched and minable quantities. One magma may produce a valuable mineral deposit of one type, and another, similar magma, may produce a mineral deposit of another type. Why this is so is not well understood; nor is it understood why most magmas produce no mineral deposits of economic value at all. Therein lies the frustrations of the economic geologist who is interested in exploring for, finding, and exploiting valuable mineral deposits.

Many geologic processes are involved in concentrating the chemical ingredients in a magma. One that seems to have been at work in southern Illinois about 100 million years ago is known as the hydrothermal process, hydrothermal simply meaning hot water. As much as 10 percent of a magma is thought to consist of hot water, dissolved gases, and the rarer chemical elements, especially those with low melting points.

During the early history of the magma, the materials of the hydrothermal fluid are disseminated throughout the magma. But when the magma rises to levels of lesser pressure and lower temperature in the Earth's crust, the common rock-forming minerals such as the feldspars and quartz crystallize to form such common igneous rocks as granite and gabbro. The removal of these minerals from the magma, and the elements that they contain, permits the concentration of those elements that remain. At this point the solution is defined as the hydrothermal fluid. In due course, the hydrothermal fluid may be forced under considerable pressure into the surrounding rock. If the surrounding rock is porous and happens to be chemically reactive, such as a permeable limestone, the invading hydrothermal fluid may be especially apt to form new mineral concentrations.

As stated previously, many hydrothermal fluids consist not only of water and dissolved gases but may be rich in metallic elements of low-melting values, especially fluorine, zinc, lead, and barium. These metallic elements with low-melting points were present in the original magma all along. But they were widely dispersed and "lost" in the original magma. It is in the hydrothermal fluid that they become concentrated. As the minerals containing elements of higher melting points are removed from the magma through cooling and solidification, elements with low melting points remain. In this way, fluorine, zinc, lead, barium, potassium, magnesium, cadmium, calcium, germanium, gold, silver, and other metallic elements, as well as the fluorides, tellurides, arsenides, and sulfur dioxide, are increasingly concentrated.

When the hydrothermal fluids—sometimes called mineralizing solutions—are expelled under great pressure into the surrounding rock, a continuing sequence of complicated chemical events takes place. In southern Illinois, some of the mineral-rich fluids were forced into pre-existing fissures and fractures already present in the Mississippian-aged limestones. If the rock had not been extensively fractured and faulted before the hydrothermal fluids were emplaced, and if the rock had been other than limestone, it is questionable if the mineralizing solutions would have been effective. But the strata were fractured by previous structural movements, and the hydrothermal solutions invaded limestone, so mineral deposition—in this case, fluorite deposition—began.

Although hydrothermal solutions occur under high pressure at great depth, these fluids, in their upward journey, pass through various zones of lowered pressure that promote the precipitation of minerals. Constrictions in channelways, for example, or partial filling of a fracture by an earlier phase of mineral deposition, or other barriers, may cause excess pressure to build up. The escape of mineralizing solutions to open areas above the constrictions lowers the pressure and promotes deposition. Thus, physical changes in the openings through which solutions pass may localize the deposition of minerals from hydrothermal solutions. In this way, some fissures may be devoid of any mineralization while nearby fractures are richly filled with the sought-after minerals. For this reason, the exploration for and mining of economic minerals is difficult, frustrating, uncertain, and expensive.

Ample room in the fissures and fault fractures provides the opportunity for mineral deposition, especially for crystal formation. Fluorite readily develops its characteristic cubic-crystal shape, and crystallized galena, sphalerite, and barite are seen inextricably associated with the fluorite in what is called the fissure, or vein-type, deposit. The deposits in and around Rosiclare primarily are the emplaced vein-type deposit and amply fill the previously open fractures with a mineral wealth that to this day stands unsurpassed. Crude ore entering the mill from the Rosiclare district, for instance, averages about 50 percent fluorite, 1.3 percent lead, and 0.3 percent zinc.

The bedded fluorite ore deposits that predominate in Cave-In-Rock district formed in a different manner than that of the vein deposit just described for the Rosiclare district. A process of replacement occurred. Pre-existing rock was replaced by fluorite, galena, and other minerals. For replacement to have occurred, the invading hydrothermal solutions must have encountered chemically unstable minerals. In this case, the presence of calcite in the limestone was central to the process. It first allowed chemical substitution to take place and then replacement ensued. Calcite was exchanged with fluorite and the resulting fluorite ore body occupied the same volume and retained the same shape and structure as the original limestone body.

In a way, the resulting ore is like a brick wall in which the bricks were removed one by one and a silver brick, for instance, of similar size and shape was substituted for each removed brick in the wall. The new wall was of the same size and form, with the same brick pattern but it was composed of silver instead of clay. This is how replacement proceeds, except that the parts interchanged are infinitesimally small, of molecular or atomic size.

Replacement necessarily involves a continuous supply of new material and removal of dissolved materials. Although fluorite-bearing solutions in southern Illinois passed through and replaced much of the calcite present in the limestone—and thereby altering the limestone—the solutions did not enter the overlying sandstone layers. Two reasons account for the absence of fluorite in the sandstone layers. First, sandstones in the southern Illinois mining district apparently were neither sufficiently porous nor possessed a network of interconnecting openings through which the mineralizing fluids could travel. Second, and more importantly, the chemical properties of limestone made it more susceptible to replacement by ore-bearing solutions than most other rock types. Yet, it must be pointed out that all limestones are not equally susceptible to ore depositions. Acids, such as hydrochloric and hydrofluoric, play a crucial role in the chemistry of ore development in limestone, which is a carbonate sedimentary rock that potentially is highly responsive and reactive to these acids.

The limestone being invaded must not be in chemical balance with the invading solutions. In an unbalanced chemical state, the limestone exerts a profound effect on the course of mineral deposition by the hydrothermal solution. Hydrochloric acid in particular plays a key role, and under certain chemical conditions when the acid is weak, the hydrothermal solution can pass through a sequence of carbonate rocks with little reaction. So, even if limestones are present, hydrothermal solutions might not react with them at all, and ore deposition will not take place. Hydrothermal solutions in many instances seem to have a peculiar propensity in by-passing certain carbonate rocks and replacing others. With the present state of knowledge about the complex chemistry of hydrothermal solutions, it is not readily understood why certain beds are more selectively mineralized than others. The selective replacement of specific rock formations is a subject of intense study, observation, and speculation; for therein lies the answer as to why some hydrothermal solutions invading limestone regions form valuable mineral deposits and others do not. This question remains to be answered and stands as one of the key mysteries in understanding ore deposition processes. One hundred million years ago, in what is today southern Illinois and adjacent Kentucky, geologic conditions were ideal for the formation of one of the world's richest fluorite deposit.

Much has been said so far about the igneous origin—via the hydrothermal mineralizing fluids—of fluorite. Is the igneous rock, from which the mineralizing fluids may have originated, seen in and around the mining district? Is there observable evidence of igneous activity in the region? The answer to both questions is yes.

Small, isolated outcroppings of igneous rock can be seen at the surface, and additional exposures are uncovered while drilling in some of the mines (Fig. 7-4). Two kinds of igneous rocks prevail in the fluorite district, neither

Fig. 7-4. Outcrops of igneous rock are rare in the fluorite district. This peridotite outcrop, the Absher Dike, occurs along the northwestern margin of the district near Absher, Williamson County. A dike is a flat layer of intrusive igneous rock. As magma, it cut across the layering of the existing strata. (Photograph courtesy of Illinois State Geological Survey)

of which are of the more common and familiar types. One is mica-peridotite; the other is lamprophyre. Both are dark gray or greenish gray, and the principal minerals they contain are brown mica and pyroxene. Olivine, another principal mineral, is absent in the lamprophyre, but in the mica-peridotite, the olivine almost always has been altered to either serpentine or chlorite minerals. The scattered outcroppings of these igneous rocks are shown in Figure 7-5.

Figure 7-5 also shows the conspicuous elliptical pattern identified as Hicks Dome, an upward buckling of about 4,000 feet of the sedimentary strata. Normal surface erosion has stripped away much of the strata in the central area of the dome, producing an obvious "bulls-eye" appearance. Hicks Dome not only is complexly faulted but in its central area are found scattered outcroppings of mica-peridotite and lamprophyre. Although igneous activity is thought to be responsible for producing the dome, several other arguments have been offered to explain its specific origin. Some like to think the dome was formed by violent gaseous explosions associated with a deeper body of magma. These gaseous eruptions not only lifted the strata to their present domal configuration but extensively fractured and faulted the strata as well. Indeed, the extensive fracturing of the sedimentary strata was not only related to the extensive faulting but to the development of breccias, a type of rock mass composed of large, angular, and broken rocks fragmented together. Much of the brecciated areas contain abundant fluorite.

Geologic features such as Hicks Dome often are referred to as cryptoexplosive structures. Only about eight cryptoexplosive structures are known to exist in the United States. While some geologists consider them the result of meteorite impact, most think they form by sudden volcanic explosions accompanied by the powerful release of energy—even though no other surface manifestations of extrusive volcanic activity such as lava flows are evident at any cryptoexplosive structure. Passing locally through the sedimentary strata, this energy created intense shock waves of disturbance, faulting, and brecciation. Periodotite and lamprophyre emanating from the main and deeper magma chamber then traveled up along the fault zones within the cryptoexplosive structure and solidified into their present positions. These are two rare kinds of igneous rock, unusually rich in iron- and magnesium-bearing minerals. These igneous rocks are thought to make up the deep mantle below the crust. Portions of a few of these igneous rock bodies subsequently were uncovered by natural erosion.

Others consider the dome to be part of the original solidified magma chamber, an intruded igneous rock body that extends unseen for many miles in all directions at considerable depth. From it stemmed the mineralizing solutions while still in the molten, or partially solidified, state. Only the tops of these now-solidified mineralizing solutions are exposed.

Since the Precambrian, igneous activity, whether volcanic or intrusive,

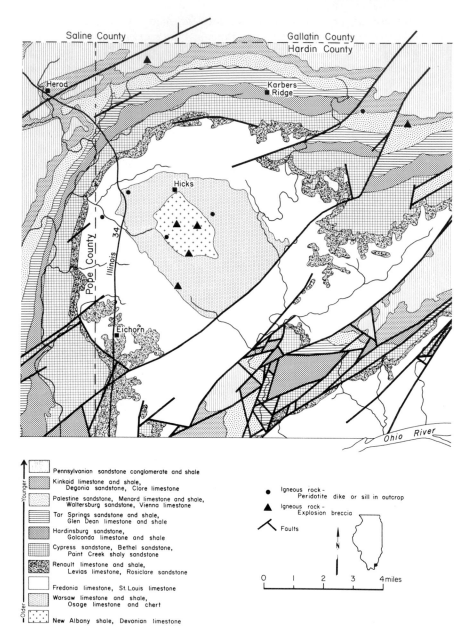

Fig. 7-5. Geologic map of the fluorite district in southern Illinois. Except for the New Albany Shale, which is Devonian in age, all other named formations are Mississippian. Note the circular "bulls-eye" pattern of Hicks Dome. The oldest, Devonian strata lie in the center while the youngest, Pennsylvanian strata are evident on the western and northern flanks. Some of the faults may have facilitated the deposition of fluorite. (Map courtesy of Illinois State Geological Survey)

has played a minor role in the overall development of the geology and topography of Illinois over the past hundreds of millions of years. Outcroppings and other occurrences of igneous rock are exceedingly rare in Illinois, and neither majestic volcanoes nor remnants of them or their ancient lava flows grace the Illinois countryside. But, for a brief geologic moment, about 100 million years ago, igneous activity may have dominated geologic events in southern Illinois and adjacent Kentucky and left the highly prized fluorite mineral assemblage and Hicks Dome.

Chapter 8
70 Million Years Ago:
The Lands Take on New Form

Missing completely in Illinois, both on the surface and in the subsurface, are strata laid down during the Permian, Triassic, and Jurassic periods. As pointed out in the beginning of the previous chapter, some unconsolidated, silty sand layers of Cretaceous age occur in extreme southern Illinois, and similar layers are locally present in western Illinois.

Although the Permian strata are absent in the Midwest, evidence elsewhere in the United States suggests that Permian seas indeed may have covered much of Illinois at this time. Sediments from these seas would have been laid down about 250 million years ago. Assuming that these sediments were deposited in Illinois, the absence of Permian strata in the state is probably due in part to removal by post-Permian erosion. No evidence exists to suggest that extensive deposits, either marine or continental, accumulated in Illinois during the subsequent Triassic and Jurassic periods. Perhaps strata of Triassic and Jurassic ages were present in Illinois and subsequently removed by erosion. The evidence seems to suggest that, more likely, they simply were never laid down, that a sea did not cover Illinois during those times.

Cretaceous rocks in southern Illinois—in Pope, Massac, Pulaski, Alexander, and Union counties—lie at the north end of the broad Mississippi Embayment of the Gulf Coastal Plain Province (Figures 8-1 and 10-4). They are poorly consolidated, clastic sediments and represent the nonmarine, or continental, part of a large delta built into the embayment by a river entering from the east. These clastic sediments predate those being laid

Facing page. The very fine sand in this abandoned pit is the late Cretaceous McNairy Formation. About 70 million years old, the McNairy Formation is exposed in the Coastal Plain Province at Fayville, Alexander County. The sand was used to meet Federal Government specifications for making dense, special-purpose concrete.

down by the modern Mississippi River that today enters the same embayment from the north. The Cretaceous sediments contain a high content of heavier trace minerals, such as kyanite, staurolite, tourmaline, sillimanite, zircon, and rutile, found principally in metamorphic rocks. Their presence indicates that the sediments were derived from a metamorphic terrain, the closest being the Precambrian highlands of the eastern Piedmont region of the Carolinas. About 500 feet thick near Cairo in Alexander County, the Cretaceous sediments thin rapidly northward where they are overlain by sediments of younger Tertiary age.

In western Illinois, the Cretaceous sediments are only about 100 feet thick and are also clastic, being composed largely of sands. Unlike their equivalents in southern Illinois, the Cretaceous sediments of western Illinois are not part of the Mississippi Embayment but rather the easternmost outliers of contemporary sediments that at one time covered the entire region east of the Rocky Mountains and north of the Missouri Ozarks. In Illinois, these erosional remnants, or outliers as they are better known, are nearly 200 miles from the closest Cretaceous exposures in west-central Iowa. They appear to be beach and nearshore sediments laid down by an advancing Cretaceous sea.

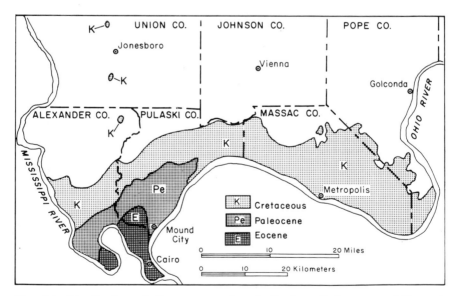

Fig. 8-1. Distribution of Cretaceous and early Tertiary (Paleocene and Eocene) strata of the Coastal Plain in southern Illinois. (Illustration courtesy of Illinois State Geological Survey)

Little changed during the succeeding Tertiary time. Sediments continued to be deposited in the Mississippi Embayment, and near Cairo these sediments are about 400 feet thick. The earlier of these are largely soft marine clays and sands, but the sands and silty clays deposited later in the Tertiary Period indicate a return to a nonmarine delta as had existed during the Cretaceous Period. Progressive subsidence of the embayment, perhaps in response to the weight of the accumulating sediments, resulted in a thickening of both the Cretaceous and Tertiary deposits toward the south. Sinking of the embayment also established a southward dip somewhat greater than that seen in the sediments of late Tertiary age.

Unfortunately, fossil evidence from the Cretaceous and Tertiary of Illinois is limited. It includes a few plant fossils found in some of the lignite beds. In other formations are found microfossils of foramanifera and radiolaria, that is, small, microscopic, single-celled marine organisms. Elsewhere, the fossil evidence includes fish scales and shark teeth and the impressions, either casts or molds, of pelecypods and gastropods.

Fig. 8-2. The early Tertiary, Porters Creek Clay exposed in this active pit at Olmstead, Pulaski County, is useful for its special ability to absorb grease and oil. Such a clay is known as "fuller's earth" and at Olmstead is mined principally as a cat box filler and sold as Kitty Litter.

Although the fossil record from these two time periods might be considered unspectacular, some of the early Tertiary sediments are of commercial value. Certain fine-grained clays have special absorptive and filtering properties and are known as fuller's earth. These have long been exploited at Olmstead, Illinois, about 20 miles north of Cairo in Pulaski County near the Ohio River (Fig. 8-2). Fuller's earth differs from ordinary clay by having a higher percentage of water and by lacking plasticity, which is the ability to be molded and formed when wet. In England, the term was originally applied to clay used for fulling wool, that is, removing the natural oils and greases from sheep's wool. Later, this clay was discovered to have the ability to remove unwanted colors from oils, and petroleum companies used it to decolorize various oil products. Fuller's earth is used also for medicinal purposes; in the manufacture of wallpaper pigments and talcum powder substitute; and to clarify and filter animal, vegetable, and mineral oils, fats, and greases.

In 1947 it was discovered that the absorptive and filtering properties of the early Tertiary clays from Olmstead made this material useful as cat-box filler. And an industry emerged in the Olmstead area in which fuller's earth is marketed commercially as "Kitty Litter." Variations in clay composition and in the amounts and types of deodorizers added to the clay have produced a variety of label brands.

Near the end of the Tertiary Period, less than 15 million years ago, Illinois was slowly taking on a subdued topographic profile. Lying between the Appalachian and Rocky mountains, the great rivers from the north, east, and west came together in the low-lying and relatively featureless Illinois Basin to flow southward into the sea. But these rivers did not everywhere follow the present and familiar lines of drainage. Within the next few million years, a new event, one of far-reaching impact, an event unlike any that had shaped Illinois in the past, would profoundly alter the face of the Midwest. The climate would get colder, and wetter, nourishing immense glaciers. These would sweep into the region from the north and northeast and rearrange the landscape on a grand scale. Rivers would be diverted and existing valleys abandoned and buried under glacial sediment. Flooding glacial meltwater would erode new channels across the region where none had been before. The exceptionally wide Cache Valley, for example, north of Horseshoe Lake in Alexander County, and mentioned in Chapter 3, is as much as four miles wide and is thought to be the former valley of the Ancient Ohio River (Fig. 8-3). The present, tiny river could not have carved a valley as wide as the one seen today. And flooding meltwaters probably forced the Mississippi River to turn sharply southward through a shallow valley at Thebes, through the rock-floored Thebes Gorge, and caused it also to abandon its original, late Tertiary, much-wider valley to the west.

But these are changes in the landscape and in the drainage pattern that are to occur in the Pleistocene Epoch. In the meantime, the small mammals that had appeared earlier in the Mesozoic were rapidly evolving into a wide variety of species and sizes both on the lands and in the seas; birds were taking on new forms; dinosaurs and the other great saurians of the lands, seas, and the air had vanished; and flower-bearing rather than cone-bearing plants increasingly dominated the landscapes of North America and the world.

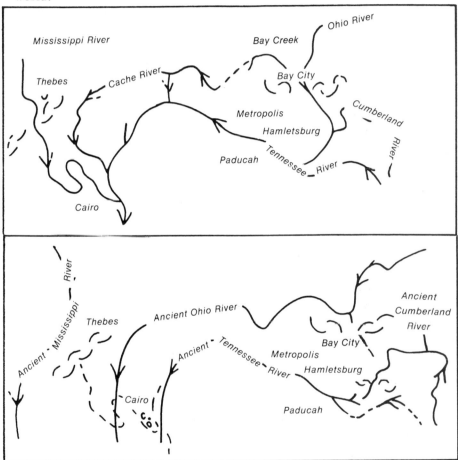

Fig. 8-3. Present drainage *(above)* and late Tertiary drainage *(below)* in southern Illinois. The Ohio River during late Tertiary time flowed through the Cache Valley, and the Mississippi River flowed through a wide and deep valley west of Thebes into southeastern Missouri and northeastern Arkansas. North of Thebes, the Mississippi River today turns southeast, abandoning its wide valley, and flows through a narrow bedrock channel, the Thebes Gorge, to its junction with the Ohio River at Cairo. These changes in the late Tertiary drainage pattern were caused by floods of glacial meltwater during the Ice Ages.

Chapter 9
Three Million Years Ago:
The Great Ice Ages

Of all the geologic changes known to have occurred during Earth's long history, the Ice Ages of the Pleistocene Epoch are among the most intriguing. The two more recent of these left an impressive legacy: Lake Michigan and the other Great Lakes, the exceptionally fertile till plains of mid-America, and the serrated landscape of the high western Rocky Mountains. Even the disappearance of such impressive prehistoric beasts as the mammoth, sabercat, mastodon, ground sloth, and long-horned bison may be attributed to glaciation. In spite of the effects the Pleistocene glaciers have had on the lands over which they passed, and on the plant and animal inhabitants, details of their origin remain to this day one of the great debates of natural science.

Worldwide glaciation was not restricted only to the Pleistocene Epoch. Vast sheets of glacial ice spread across large areas of the continents at other times in the geologic past, although no evidence for them are known from Illinois. At least one ice age occurred late in the Precambrian Era, about 700 million years ago, and three since then, one in the Ordovician Period, another in the Pennsylvanian Period, and the third in the Pleistocene for which a good record is present in Illinois. Whether worldwide glaciation of Earth is a cyclic phenomenon is difficult to say; the time intervals between these recognized events are far too irregular. But one fact can be stated with certainty: episodes of continental glaciation have been rare events in the sum total of Earth history. Therefore, it is inferred that the glaciation cycles required a special combination of climatic and environmental conditions. Clearly, the relationship between the growth of ice sheets and a cooling of the world climate is an obvious one. Consequences of a new ice age in the future include drastic shifts in the ability to produce corn, wheat, and other

Facing page. Loess, a wind-blown sediment of glacial origin, exposed at Chester, Randolph County.

agricultural products and profoundly negative effects on almost every major city. The causes for the onset of glaciation, therefore, are intensely studied by climatologists and glaciologists.

During the latter part of the Cenozic Era the warm equitable climate of the Mesozoic Era began to cool. Geologic evidence indicates that the strong temperature zonation of tropical, temperate, and polar climates evident today was not present either in Mesozoic or in early Cenozoic time. The trend toward such pronounced temperature zonation began later in the Cenozoic and is marked by the disappearance of plants and animals adapted to warm environments, first in high and then in low latitudes. The conditions that brought about these changes are not well understood.

Exploration of high-latitude lands such as Antarctica and Alaska has established that glaciation in these regions began at least five million years ago—perhaps even earlier. Prior to the recent discovery that the Pleistocene Ice Ages began at least three million years ago, it was thought that all the geologically recent glaciations were contained within only the last million years. Despite this refrigeration of Arctic and Antarctic lands—and high mountain regions also—there is no evidence that continental ice sheets extended into the middle latitudes until about three million years ago (Fig. 9-1). Then, a major part of North America and much of Eurasia was invaded by ice sheets as thick as, or thicker than, the 8,000-foot-thick glacial cover occupying Antarctica today. A maximum of at least nine million square miles, from New York City westward to St. Louis and Seattle, as well as nearly all of Canada, was under ice as recently as 20,000 years ago; in Europe the ice sheets spread as far south as Copenhagen, Berlin, and Leningrad. Today in the United States, exclusive of Alaska, only 20 cubic miles of glaciers remain—in the higher elevations of the Rocky Mountains.

Since the last half of the 19th century, geologists have known that the thick glacial ice sheets advanced and then retreated several times across North America. Each ice advance and each retreat formed within the Pleistocene a distinct interval known as a glacial or an interglacial stage. The evidence for such repetitive glacial stages is recorded in the overlapping layers of different tills deposited by the former ice sheets. Till is a sediment deposit picked up by a glacier from the terrain over which it moves and consists largely of a mixture of clay, sand, gravel, and boulders varying widely in size and shape (Fig. 9-2).

These materials, frozen in the ice, may be transported hundreds of miles. When deposited as the glacier melts, they generally are both unconsolidated and unstratified. Till is deposited directly, that is, the sediment particles are not moved elsewhere by glacial melt-water. Younger, overlying layers of till appear less weathered in contrast to the older tills that lie beneath (Fig. 9-3). During the tens of thousands of years of an interglacial stage, the upper ten feet or so of till deposited by the previous ice sheet has sufficient time to weather, discolor, and either chemically reduce or oxidize. These processes are part of soil formation. Indeed, the till may develop

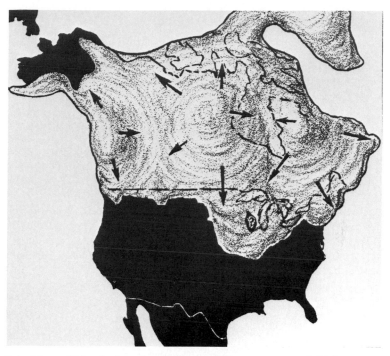

Fig. 9-1. Map of North America showing maximum extent of Pleistocene glaciations. Note the location of the Wisconsin Driftless Section, shown with a ? and the southernmost penetration of the glacier on the continent in Illinois. (J. J. Fagan, *View of the Earth: An Introduction to Geology,* Holt, Rinehart and Winston, Inc., 1965, p. 328, reprinted by permission of CBS College Publishing)

unusual properties as a consequence of the long weathering process, especially when it is composed primarily of clay undergoing chemical reduction in a poorly drained and wet environment.

One example is gley, sometimes called "gumbo" by farmers in Iowa, Illinois, and thereabouts (Fig. 9-4). When damp, gleyed clay is sticky, impervious to fluids, and resembles wet starch. In such a condition it is particularly plastic, that is, easily shaped and molded in the hands. When dry, this same material hardens like concrete. This gray to dark-colored clay represents one of the horizons of a well-developed soil that formed during the millennia on the depressions and flat surfaces of the older till before it was buried beneath a younger one.

Early studies of North American geology indicated that at least four major glacial stages occurred, with varyingly long, intervening, ice-free stages. More recent information, however, obtained especially from analyses of a large number of deep-sea cores, indicates that at least eight, perhaps nine, major changes in climate, rather than the four usually described, occurred during the last 850,000 years; perhaps as many as 26 oscillations between cold and warm climates may have taken place. Deep-

Fig. 9-2. Immense boulders, torn from the bedrock by glaciers, were transported hundreds of miles by the ice before being deposited as part of the till. Conspicuous, isolated boulders are called erratics. This one, southwest of Kankakee, is three feet in height and composed of Precambrian granite from Canada. (Photograph courtesy of Illinois State Geological Survey)

Fig. 9-3. Nearly 90 percent of Illinois was covered at least once by continental glaciers. Two episodes of glaciation are evident at this well-known exposure in a railroad cut a mile east of Farmdale, Tazewell County. After the older Illinoian Till **(G)** was deposited, an interval of physical and chemical weathering produced the deep Sangamon Soil **(S)**. Wind-blown loess and silt **(Mr)** eventually covered this soil. Thick Wisconsinan Till **(Wd)** then covered these earlier deposits. Last to accumulate after withdrawal of the Wisconsinan ice sheet was the youngest loess **(R)**. (Photograph courtesy of Illinois State Geological Survey)

Fig. 9-4. One of the best-preserved exposures of gleyed clay is seen in an embankment near Effingham, Effingham County. The head of the 30-inch-long pick identifies the top of the gley, which continues downward beyond the hammer for several feet. Once called "gumbo," this clay was derived by chemical reduction (or gleying) on a poorly drained surface after the withdrawal of the Illinoian glacier and during the formation of the Sangamon Soil (Fig. 9-3). Wind-blown loess then accumulated over the gley. (Photograph courtesy of Illinois State Geological Survey)

sea sediments contain a more complete geologic record than sediments deposited on the continents because the oceanic environment is more protective. The sediments are not ravaged by erosion and other destructive processes as are those exposed on the continents.

Re-examination of numerous localities in mid-America, New England, and elsewhere and more detailed studies of the glacial and interglacial deposits reinforce the idea that more than four episodes of continent-wide glaciation affected North America, Europe, and Asia. Nevertheless, geoscientists in North America, by "lumping" the major oscillations of the glaciers, continue to refer to four basic glacial stages during the Pleistocene. Beginning with the earliest, these are the Nebraskan, Kansan, Illinoian, and the Wisconsinan. The three interglacial stages that separate the glacial stages are, again beginning with the earliest, the Aftonian, Yarmouthian, and Sangamonian. Although date correlations are somewhat controversial and inconclusive, it is generally agreed that the Nebraskan Glaciation began between 2 and 3 million years ago and ended about 1.7 million years ago; the Kansan extended from 1.4 million years ago to about 950,000 years ago; the Illinoian from about 500,000 years ago to 125,000 years ago; and the Wisconsinan Glaciation from about 75,000 years ago to about 10,000 years ago.

The names are derived from geographic areas where the respective till deposit of that glacial stage, or the soil developed during the interglacial stage, was first studied and described. Generally, these areas coincide with areas where the respective tills or soils are best developed. "Nebraskan" was proposed for the lowermost till exposed at Afton Junction and Thayer in Union County, Iowa, based on its supposed extension into nearby eastern Nebraska. The "Illinoian" was named for the state that marks the southernmost penetration of any of the glacial stages into the United States, reaching a latitude of 37°30′N. More than 100 feet of till thickness from this glacial stage is also found in Illinois. The Sangamonian Interglacial was identified on the basis of a prominent and recognizable soil, including the gleyed clay that developed in deeply weathered Illinoian-age till, and described from several hand-dug water wells in Sangamon County, Illinois. The Wisconsinan is named after the state of Wisconsin where the youngest till and other glacial deposits are so well developed. Although the type localities for each deposit are geographically restricted, the names are applied throughout North America.

Except for the southernmost seven counties, Jo Daviess, and part of Carroll counties in the northwestern corner of the state, Illinois owes its present surface configuration almost entirely to the movements and activities of the last two glacial stages, the Illinoian and the Wisconsinan (Fig. 3-4). The effects of each of the two major glaciations are easily identified by an examination of the regional terrain, and the boundary between their respective areas usually is readily apparent.

Wisconsinan glacial topography displays a comparatively new, less-weathered, and less-modified appearance when compared to the older Illinoian surface. For example, the Wisconsinan Till Plain is interrrupted by a minimum of 32 morainal ridges, or low rises, in the landscape composed of till. These moraines mark the former positions of the ice front, and they are arranged in conspicuously concentric arcs that follow the rounded edge of Lake Michigan. The moraines are about two miles wide and not more than 50 feet high with intervening valleys several miles wide between some of them. The hummocky terrain of low till ridges and intervening swales is especially evident south and west of Chicago (Fig. 9-5). During Wisconsinan time the climate cycled between cold and warm with 32 rapid reversals and readvances of the ice front. Studies of these morainal deposits indicate that fluctuations occurred between about 20,000 and 14,000 years ago. On the average, each cycle lasted about 200 years, and the ice front moved a total distance of about 900 miles in a net retreat of 200 miles. Moraines such as these are rare on the older Illinoian surface where they were either poorly developed or have been reduced by erosion during the intervening Sangamonian Interglacial Stage.

Numerous small lakes, ponds, swamps, and bogs occur in depressions in the moraine-dominated landscape of the Wisconsinan. Many of these depressions are called kettles. These were formed by the melting of large detached blocks of glacier ice that had been wholly or partly buried in glacial till. One of the finest examples is Volo Bog near Crystal Lake in McHenry County (Fig. 9-6). Here is found one of the better sediment records of any undisturbed bog. Detailed studies of its sediment content by Illinois State Museum scientists have shed considerable light in reconstructing the late Pleistocene climate and environment, especially of the kinds of plants living in the region from about 10,000 years ago until the mid-1800s.

Fig. 9-5. The forest-covered Cary Moraine of the Valparaiso Morainic System at Moraine Hills State Park, McHenry County. (Photograph courtesy of Illinois State Geological Survey)

The Illinoian Till Plain, on the other hand, is distinguished by a flatness comparable to most dry lake plains. Over many thousands of square miles the till plain is so flat—local relief in places is only 6 feet per mile—that it resembles the open ocean from horizon to horizon. Unlike the well-developed moraines on the Wisconsinan surface, moraines on the Illinoian surface are poorly preserved. Streams, however, are better established on the Illinoian surface than on the Wisconsinan because they have had more time to develop and adjust. The drainage system has had more time to mature to the point where streams do not flow into, through,

Fig. 9-6. Aerial view of Volo Bog (arrow). Formerly a much-larger kettle lake (defined by the dark, oblong area), Volo Bog has filled with sediments over the centuries, and only a small remnant of the original lake contains water. (Photograph courtesy of Illinois Department of Transportation, Aerial Surveys Division)

or out of lakes and swamps as frequently as they do on the Wisconsinan surface. Kettles, which are so common in the Wisconsinan terrain, are rare on the Illinoian surface.

The earlier Illinoian ice sheet penetrated much farther into Illinois than did the Wisconsinan. It reached the northern slopes of the Shawnee Hills deep in southern Illinois. Nearly 90 percent of the state was covered by ice at this time. Whether the Illinoian glacier could have moved even farther south is hard to say. The Shawnee Hills may have been a barrier. Or the ice front, having reached a latitude of almost 37°N, could not advance farther because of the much warmer climate in the region. In contrast to the Illinoian ice sheet, the younger Wisconsinan ice sheet occupied only about 50 percent of the state. Its southernmost position is marked by a series of low moraines around Pekin and Peoria and southward to Decatur. Known as the Shelbyville Morainic System, the moraines mark the terminal, or end, of the Wisconsinan ice sheet.

Neither the Illinoian nor the Wisconsinan Till Plain surfaces are influenced by the underlying bedrock; they represent almost exclusively a depositional topography. The incredibly low relief of the Illinoian Till Plain is a matter of some speculation, and the expansive flatness seems to be related in some measure to the physical character of the till itself. The bedrock of the Central Lowland, the primary source of the till, is predominantly limestone, dolomite, shale, and minor amounts of sandstone. Till composition studies have shown that as much as half the materials were transported from bedrock sources no more than 100 miles distant. Rock types such as these produce pebbly tills of silt and clay rather than tills containing boulders and cobbles of hard granite or metamorphic rock as seen in New England, for example. Clayey tills are sufficiently plastic and mobile to slide and spread easily at the time of deposition—at least so it is thought. Reconstruction of the preglacial terrain indicates a relief measurable in only a few hundred feet; it is conceivable that such a landscape could be leveled by the filling of its valleys rather than the erosion of its hilltops. Since the building of the till plains was a cumulative process and the product of at least two glaciations, each glacial event in some degree obliterated the older, preglacial, stream-carved topography.

Covering these till deposits in some areas is another sedimentary deposit with a strikingly different character and history. It is called loess, a term obtained from the German meaning "loose" and used by peasants and brickworkers along the Rhine Valley to describe this particular material (Fig. 9-7). Loess is indeed a loose, or unconsolidated, fine-grained, and unlayered sediment that consists of dust-sized particles of angular quartz, feldspar, mica, and other minerals mixed with traces of clay minerals. Carbonate materials serve as a weak cement. Distinctively buff to light yellow and yellowish-brown in color, loess often contains the fossils of land snails and occasionally the bones and teeth of small and large terrestrial mammals. It is traversed by a network of many small, narrow, vertical tubes left by successive generations of plant roots.

Exposures of unconsolidated or poorly cemented sediments normally erode quickly into gentle slopes. They have little cohesive strength. But loess deposits will stand in vertical cliffs, especially in dry areas. These often are tens of feet high both in naturally exposed cliffs, that stay reasonably dry, or in manmade highway and railroad cuts. This unique characteristic of loess is attributed to its high moist-to-dry strength, (that is, it is strong when dry but weak when wet), a vertically oriented internal structure defined by the narrow root tubes, an angular rather than a rounded shape of the particles, and a carbonate cement. Loess is thickest along the Mississippi, Illinois, and Missouri river valleys where it occurs as a blanket of more or less uniform thickness—usually no more than 30 feet—draped over hills and valleys alike. Thickness of the loess is greatest along the eastern uplands of the river valleys and decreases rapidly farther to the east (Fig. 9-8).

The origin of loess has been a matter of some conjecture, but it is now generally agreed that the silty sediments were stripped by winds from the bare, wide, glacial outwash floodplains of the Mississippi, Illinois, and Missouri rivers as the Wisconsinan ice sheet melted away. So much fine-grained sediment was carried down these rivers by meltwater during the

Fig. 9-7. Loess, as seen in this exposure at Chester in Randolph County, is an unconsolidated, wind-blown deposit that characteristically stands in near-vertical cliffs in
well-drained areas.

spring and summer thaws that the lesser discharge during the winter season
could not sweep most of these sediments onward. Strong winter winds
blowing eastward swept tons of this glacial silt from the dried out, un-
protected, and wind-exposed floodplain surfaces. Since the prevailing wind
direction was toward the east, loess thickness is greatest along the eastern
side of the river floodplains and decreases rapidly farther to the east as the
ancient winds quickly dropped their sediment load.

The clouds of dust that presently hang over so many of the glacially
deposited surfaces in Alaska on bright, breezy days in winter vividly
demonstrate today how easily and quickly wind is able to gather up fresh
silt. Anyone who has traveled on unpaved roads over glacial outwash-
covered surfaces of Alaska or Canada knows firsthand the nature of the
fine-textured, all-pervading, wind-susceptible soil. And no one had to teach
dust-bowl farmers about dust deposits in the 1930s as their houses and crops
were buried by fine-grained sediment and they were driven from their farms
like the Joads in John Steinbeck's "Grapes of Wrath." Accumulation of
the loess in the winter months, when much of the glacial outwash dried out,
is thought to have occurred in much the same way. Only a few hundredths
of an inch per year is all that may have been laid down. The grass and other
vegetation growing on the surface, as well as the abundant and diversified
snail fauna contained within this ancient wind-blown dust, were able to survive this accumulation and were thus unaffected.

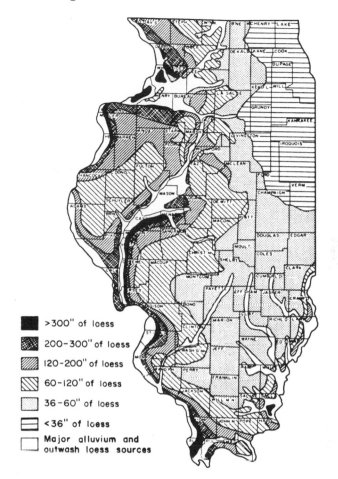

Fig. 9-8. Approximate loess depth on nearly level, uneroded topography. In such areas, loess varies from as much as 100 feet thick on the eastern bluffs overlooking major valleys to one or two feet in areas farthest from the valleys. (Map courtesy of Illinois State Geological Survey)

The loess of Illinois and adjacent states is highly desirable as productive agricultural soil. It is friable and permeable to water with good moisture-holding capacity; has a moderate density, medium texture, and a balanced mineral content; and contains no rocks that might interfere with extensive and large-scale mechanized cultivation. Indeed, without it and the presence of nearly level depositional till plains, as well as a favorable climate, it is doubtful that Illinois, heart of the Corn Belt of the United States, would have become one of the richest food-producing regions of the world.

As the Wisconsinan ice sheet spread beyond its Arctic source and entered the Midwest, it did not everywhere bury the lands beneath its massive load. Moving glacial ice behaves somewhat like a fluid and will take the path of least resistance. It will follow whatever lowlands and valleys it may encounter or spread around bold, elevated landforms. In northern Wisconsin, an upland of Precambrian rock stands between the lowlands where Lakes Superior and Michigan now occur. As such, the upland apparently stood high enough throughout the Pleistocene to effectively deflect all oncoming ice and not be overridden, thereby escaping completely the effects of glaciation. The glaciers seemed to have passed around this topographic barrier. In moving on the glaciers did not quite close in again over the southwestern part of Wisconsin and adjacent parts of Iowa, Minnesota, and that hooklike corner of northwestern Illinois in Jo Daviess and Carroll counties.

This 20,000-square-mile region may not have been an island in a "sea" of glacier ice; instead, each of the ice sheets may have persistently moved past this topographic barrier on one side or the other at different times, glaciating all the lands around it one time or another during the Pleistocene. Today, it is known as the Driftless Area after the term "drift" that includes not only till but all other deposits of glacial origin. In addition to the absence of glacial deposits within this land tract, other evidence points to the region being untouched by glacial ice. Fragile landforms such as natural bridges, arches, buttes, and rock towers stand like isolated bowling pins ready to be knocked over by the next glacial onslaught. These could not have survived a glacial advance (Fig. 9-9).

Fig. 9-9. Delicate landforms, such as this bridge of Cambrian sandstone located in Natural Bridge State Park near Prairie du Sac, Wisconsin, are evidence that the Wisconsin Driftless Area probably remained unglaciated throughout its history.

Northwest of Madison, Wisconsin, along the eastern edge of the Driftless Area, are the famed and much-visited Wisconsin Dells. The rock-pinnacled chasms, cliffs, towers, and free-standing pillars of mid-Cambrian-aged sandstone have remained to this day, silent witnesses to a time when much of North America was smothered under ice. Nor did glaciers change the look of the land in Jo Daviess County in and around the historic town of Galena. Here is seen a ruggedness of terrain unmatched elsewhere in Illinois. Unglaciated Ordovician and Silurian limestone, dolomite, and shale crop out extensively in contrast to the till plains beyond. Bold, erosional, bedrock remnants, called mounds in this Driftless Area, include the 1,235-foot-high Charles Mound, highest topographic elevation in Illinois.

When the Wisconsinan ice sheet reached its southernmost position about 20,000 years ago, the glacial front stretched uninterrupted more than 2,000 miles across the face of the continent from the base of the Rocky Mountains in northern Montana to the Atlantic Ocean (Fig. 9-1). The margin of the ice sheet was like a huge, broad ramp covered in wintertime with a new coat of white snow and in summertime showing a sediment-rich, dirty, gray ice. It sloped upward toward the north. Seventy-five miles from its leading edge the glacier was more than a mile thick. Farther up the slope the glacier was perhaps as much as two miles thick.

An untold number of meltwater streams drained off this ice ramp, especially in summer, forming wide and relatively shallow lakes between the pulsing ice front and morainal ridges. At one stage, perhaps no more than 14,000 years ago when these lakes were at their deepest, meltwater drainage into the Wabash Valley appears to have been blocked by the ice front. The water was forced to spill through gaps in the moraines and out into the Kankakee, Vermilion, and Fox rivers that are tributary to the Illinois River. As a result, the Illinois River valley was widened as the river carried a large volume of meltwater onward to the Mississippi River and the Gulf of Mexico. In fact, so much water spilled through these gaps and passed into the Kankakee Valley, in particular, that this event has come to be called the great Kankakee Flood or Kankakee Torrent.

This tremendous outpouring drained a region of dammed glacial meltwater from southern Michigan, flowed across northwestern Indiana and northeastern Illinois, and expanded to a flood area between 5 and 12 miles wide. The outpouring was capable of moving sedimentary materials as large as small boulders. Deeply scoured areas of bedrock and midstream accumulations of angular, bouldery rubble, remain today in places in the Kankakee Valley, demonstrating not only the ability of these torrents to move small boulders, but also an ability to erode the valley down to bedrock in a short time. From the headwaters of the Illinois River to the Big Bend at Hennepin, the valley is entrenched in bedrock. Below Hennepin, the flooding torrent greatly widened the valley in the relatively soft glacial deposits, and broad erosional terraces extend downstream as far as Beards-town in Cass County.

These torrents of glacial meltwater deposited such large quantities of sand and gravel on the floors of the Illinois and Kankakee river valleys that the sediment spread over new vegetation as fast as it could become established. Broad areas of sand and gravel lay exposed to persistent wind action, and the smaller sand particles were quickly winnowed out from the coarser materials. These billowed up to form the numerous sand dunes that cover so much of these river terraces today (Fig. 9-10). In many places, the dunes migrated up the river-facing bluffs and onto the uplands east of the valleys. Indeed, absence of sand dunes on the western bluffs, as well as the notable thinness of the loess, leaves no question as to the dominance of the prevailing westerly winds that formed the dunes at the time. Almost all the dunes have subsequently been stabilized by a cover of vegetation so that today many are seen to rise between 20 and 40 feet above the general ter-rain. A few are even as high as 100 feet.

Meltwater from the Wisconsinan glacier also flowed down the Wabash and Ohio rivers carrying a tremendous volume of outwash sediments into southern Illinois. These sediments choked the two major rivers and dammed the valleys of the tributaries not directly connected with the melting glaciers. As a result, slackwater lakes were created in stopped-up river basins.

Fig. 9-10. Sand dunes, some as high as 60 feet, are preserved in the Henry Allan Gleason Nature Preserve near Havana, Mason County, along the eastern bluffs of the Illinois River.

One of these slackwater lakes, Lake Saline, periodically filled with water that laid down about 150 feet of fine-textured sediments (Fig. 9-11). Apparently the lake level fluctuated too rapidly for beaches and low wave-cut cliffs to form. Loess-covered bedrock knobs without lake deposits identify the location of islands. Sediment brought in by glacier meltwater remained in suspension for some time and was able to circulate and be eventually deposited throughout the slackwater lake basin (Fig. 9-12). Deposition of these lake sediments ended when Wabash floodwater eroded some of the sediments in the valley, allowing the slackwater lakes to drain.

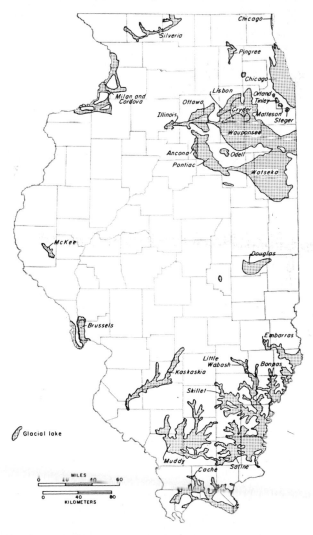

Fig. 9-11. Glacial lakes of Illinois. Glacial Lake Chicago is the forerunner of present-day Lake Michigan. (Illustration courtesy of Illinois State Geological Survey)

Fig. 9-12. Geologists examining the details of fine-textured sediments, mostly silt and clay, laid down in Glacial Lake Saline north of Eldorado, Saline County, during Wisconsinan time. (Photograph courtesy of Illinois State Geological Survey)

Apart from the bare, broad, and exposed valley floodplains, the country adjacent to the edge of the ice sheet was carpeted with tundralike plants, and scattered about here and there were small clumps of spruce trees. The tundra of today is a broadly level or slightly undulating plain in Arctic regions that supports a distinctive growth of mosses, lichens, and various low shrubs and is underlain by a dark, mucky soil and permanently frozen ground termed permafrost. Scientists who study the events of the Pleistocene Epoch agree that modern tundra is different in some ways from its Pleistocene counterpart that developed in Illinois. While permafrost prevailed, the Pleistocene tundra probably was drier and, beyond Illinois, supported animals such as horses and bison and plants that could not survive in the moist and more boggy environment of the modern tundra.

Soil typical of the tundra is not present in the sediment record except in areas that are, or were, bogs. However, some features typical of a tundra, such as pingos and frostwedges have been recognized. Pingos are large conical mounds of soil-covered ice about 10 or 15 feet high and 150 feet in diameter that are raised by hydrostatic pressure of water within the permafrost. And frost wedges are wedge-shaped masses of ice or frozen soil. Because of such features, alternative terms such as "tundralike," or "parkland," or "open ground vegetation," or "Arctic steppe" are used to describe the Pleistocene countryside near the edge of the ice sheet.

Some tundra plants, as well as other "Arctic steppe" plants, lived in Illinois during the time of glaciation. Large quantities of reproductive parts such as spores and pollen released by the plants during each growing season accumulated in nearby bogs and lakes. The generations of plants that lived and died around and near these lakes can be reconstructed in detail. This is done by drilling a core through the full thickness of peat and other sediments of these bogs and lakes and then identifying the kinds of pollen and other plant remains preserved in each layer of sediment (Fig. 9-13). What one would expect to find is a progressive change in plant life as the climate continued to gradually become warmer: first, plants typical of the tundra; then those of the fir and spruce forest; then those from a birch and pine forest; and so on to oak, beech, alder, and hazel. In other words, the tundralike zone was slowly replaced by the fir and spruce forest that had

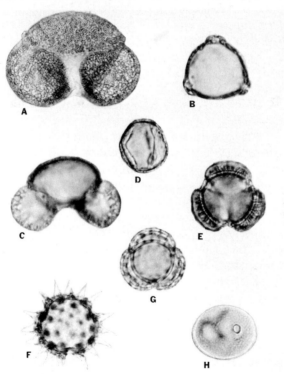

Fig. 9-13. Pollen grains of eight flowering plants and trees from the Quaternary Period. Note how each grain is distinctive. **A.** pine, *Pinus resinosa,* 82 microns long; **B.** birch, *Betula pumila,* 26 microns; **C.** pine, *Pinus banksiana,* 55 microns; **D.** white oak, *Quercus alba,* 33 microns; **E.** sagebrush, *Artemesia* sp., 27 microns; **F.** sunflower, *Helianthus annuus,* 27 microns; **G.** ragweed, *Ambrosia* sp , 21 microns; and **H.** grass, *Gramineae,* 34 microns. The micron, a unit of measurement for microscopic objects, is 1/1000 of a millimeter. (Photograph courtesy of J. King, Illinois State Museum)

been growing hundreds of miles farther south. As the climate became progressively warmer, the ice sheet continued to melt, the ice front retreating farther and farther to the north. The fir and spruce forest, also progressing northward, was replaced by the birch and pine forest, and so on.

Beginning about 15,000 years ago, the Wisconsinan ice front started its northward retreat. The adjacent tundralike zone, its soil frozen all winter and moderately wet in summer, shifted northward also. By comparing similar regions today, we can imagine how Illinois must have looked when the ice sheet lay here. During the summer months, clouds of mosquitoes and black-flies probably swarmed. The weather was persistently cloudy and cool with abundant rain and occasional snow. Winter was probably sunny and cold with frequent and heavy snowfalls. This generally cold and unsettled weather resulted from the presence of the ice sheet. Being nearly as high as the Rocky Mountains, the ice sheet constituted a significant barrier to the warmer, moist air masses persistently flowing northward and eastward from the Gulf of Mexico. Forced to rise over the thick ice sheet, these relatively warm air masses chilled quickly to form dark and heavy storm clouds that released their moisture as rain or snow.

Cold-air masses descending the mile-high ice sheet warmed considerably, just as air masses today warm when they descend a mountain range. The best examples of such warming and drying winds are the Great Plains chinooks of the eastern Rockies or the Santa Ana winds out of the Sierra Nevada of southern California. A chinook in January will raise the air temperature by as much as 50°F within two minutes as the air mass descending the mountain front is compressed by higher atmospheric pressure. To be sure, chinooks do not happen everyday; they develop under certain atmospheric conditions. But when they do occur, the effect is one of pronounced warming over a brief time span. Therefore, Pleistocene geologists again say that, paradoxically, winters at this time were probably less severe than they are today in Illinois. Low temperatures probably did not fall to such now-familiar extremes as -10°F or -20°F and midwinter high temperatures probably rose more frequently to 40°F or 50°F. Conversely, the Pleistocene summers also were much cooler.

South of the tundralike zone, the sparse and scattered clumps of spruce and fir thickened to form a continuous evergreen forest, the kind seen today in the taiga, a swampy area of coniferous forest found below the tundra of the subarctic of North America and Eurasia. Along its southerly edge, greater numbers of broad-leaf trees began to mix in with the predominant spruce and fir. Pines also were present, but the southernmost fringe of this prehistoric taiga in Illinois was almost completely without pines. On the Arctic steppe, within walking distance of the ice front, was the wooly mammoth (*Mammuthus primigenius*), largest and best known of all the tundra animals (Fig. 9-14). A short-tailed and small-eared elephant as big or bigger than its modern relative, the wooly mammoth was well equipped to stand the rigorous climate along the glacial front. Its guard hairs, 10 to 15 inches

Fig. 9-14. Reconstruction of the wooly mammoth. Although common in the Arctic steppe of northern North America, the wooly mammoth may not have ranged as far south as Illinois, where related species of mammoth are found as fossils. (Illustration courtesy of Field Museum of Natural History)

long, were interspersed with a coat of thick wool. Just beneath the skin was a layer of fat two or three inches thick, and over the skull was a fatty pad which formed a hump on the shoulders. This accumulation of fat enabled the animal to survive winter when food sources were snow-covered. Its rasplike molar teeth, with flat and reinforced grinding surfaces, were well suited for grazing on the carpet of tundra plants. Tusks often developed to enormous sizes in older individuals, were strongly recurved, and frequently even reached the ground. The worn surfaces of the tips and undersides of such tusks suggest that they were used as snowplows to clear the snow cover so the animal could feed on the low shrubs and herbaceous plants and mosses.

Mammoths ranged widely across America, from the Atlantic to the Pacific, onward across the now-submerged narrow land bridge between Alaska and Siberia; in Eurasia they ranged westward to the Atlantic again. Their fossils exist in numbers that are absolutely incredible. Tens, perhaps hundreds of thousands of mammoth tusks, ribs, skulls, jaw bones, and long bones were used by prehistoric people of the Stone Age in the construction of dwellings and settlements 35,000 to 50,000 years ago when great herds of these behemoths roamed throughout the Ukraine and southern Siberia. Numerous skeletal parts have been found where they were used at these Stone Age sites: skulls deliberately wedged into the ground as house walls; long bones used as supports for roasting spits and other structures; tusks formed into arches of roofs; skulls with tusks intact arranged into arched entryways; and shoulder blades covering grave sites or modified to serve as tools for construction. About 60,000 fossil mammoth tusks were collected before the turn of this century in Siberia alone and marketed for use as billiard balls, piano keys, chessmen, and other articles made from the highly prized ivory. Even today almost half the commercial ivory is derived from this fossil source. About 30,000 mammoths have been found at or near the surface in remote Siberia alone: one can imagine how many remain buried not only in Eurasia but also in North America as well.

Mammoth remains have been recovered at a few localities in and around the Chicago area (Fig. 9-15). Those of the Jefferson's mammoth (*Mammuthus jeffersonii*) are especially abundant in Illinois and the Midwest. Fossils from DuPage County are relatively numerous, and one of the more complete specimens was found near Golconda in Pope County. This specimen presently resides in the collections of the Illinois State Museum. In 1910, what was the largest mammoth ever found in the United States came from Kewanee, Illinois. Since then still larger individuals have been found in Nebraska and Arizona, some of which are known to have stood nearly 15 feet at the shoulder with recurved tusks measuring up to 13 feet.

Fig. 9-15. Fossils of Jefferson's mammoth are abundant in Illinois and the Midwest. The mammoth is named in honor of President Thomas Jefferson who was interested in such fossils; at the White House he kept a collection of remains of ground sloth, mammoth, mastodon, and other extinct animals. (Reconstruction by W. Stone and J. Saunders, Illinois State Museum)

In the spruce-and-fir forest zone that merged into the Arctic steppe, another elephantlike animal, the American mastodon (*Mammut americanum*) could be seen (Fig. 9-16). Whereas the mammoth was a grazer, the mastodon was a browser, preferring the trees and shrubs of the forest. The mastodon was well adapted for a life in the forest. Its distinctly high-cusped molar teeth were suited to a diet of plant matter that needed to be crushed. Smaller than the mammoth—usually about 10 feet at the shoulder—and with tusks considerably smaller in proportion to the body length, it could move between close-growing trees with much less difficulty than could the mammoth. The mastodon ranged widely through nearly all the forested parts of the United States and its fossil remains are found as far south as Florida and even central Mexico (Fig. 9-17). In Illinois, mastodon remains come largely from the Aurora area where skeletal parts, including skulls and tusks, from about 20 individuals have been uncovered. Fossil remains of two individuals are known also from Chester in Randolph County.

Fig. 9-16. An American mastodon moves across a late Pleistocene landscape of spruce and mixed deciduous forest about 16,000 years ago. In the background, two other mastodons browse on spruce trees in a low, marshy area. Dryer, adjacent areas support such deciduous trees as oak, alder, and ash. These plants, and others, are known to have grown in such a setting based on detailed studies of pollen collected from sediments. (Painting by R. Larson, Illinois State Museum)

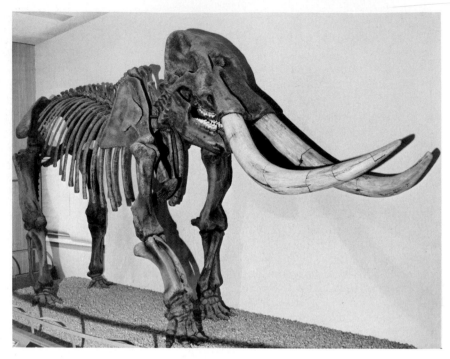

Fig. 9-17. Reassembled skeleton of the American mastodon on display in the Illinois State Museum. Consisting of skeletal parts collected at Boney Spring in western Missouri, this mastodon is one of the largest known in North America.

On the Missouri side of the Mississippi River, near the town of Kimmswick about 20 miles south of St. Louis, scientists from the Illinois State Museum uncovered the fossil bones of mastodon and other animals such as deer, the extinct long-legged stag-moose (*Cervalces scotti*), and the extinct long-nosed peccary (*Mylohyus nasutus*) in 1979 and 1980 (Fig. 9-18). That in itself, while of importance, would not be considered unusual. Unique to this site, however, was the discovery of stone tools. A projectile point beneath and in contact with a mastodon bone was also discovered, suggesting the possibility that this point had been embedded in the flesh of the animal (Fig. 9-19). The stone tools and the projectile point were typical of those made by the Clovis people. They were the first to inhabit North America and are so named for the town of Clovis, New Mexico, where the first site containing Clovis stone tools were found in association with the extinct mammoth.

At Kimmswick, at least two mastodons—not mammoths—were killed by Clovis hunters. These animals were possibly a cow and her calf, their approximate ages being determined by the wear of their teeth. Butchering and

Fig. 9-18. The Kimmswick excavation as it appeared in summer 1979. Clovis people lived at this site about 11,000 years ago. Excavated vertebrae are protected in white plaster jackets; the upside-down bucket in the center square protects a nearly complete Clovis projectile point. (Photograph by D. Hall, courtesy R. Graham, Illinois State Museum)

Fig. 9-19. A Clovis projectile point in situ at the Kimmswick Site. Numerous mastodon bones near the point had been removed before this photograph was taken. (Photograph by D. Hall, courtesy R. Graham, Illinois State Museum)

processing of these mastodons seems to have been done in specialized activity areas, indicated by the spatial distribution of the excavated bones.

Clovis artifacts have been found throughout the United States and northern Mexico, but only about 15 Clovis sites contain the necessary sediment records with fossil remains of animals to permit reconstruction and interpretation of the lifeways of these people. All such sites are restricted to the Great Plains and the southwestern United States where they are associated with the remains of mammoths. This relationship between the Clovis people and mammoths has led some scholars to suggest that the Clovis people were specifically hunting mammoths. The excavations at Kimmswick, therefore, are of particular importance in that they provide the first evidence of Clovis people hunting the mastodon rather than the mammoth. In addition, the excavations provide the first opportunity to analyze how the Clovis people adapted to the late Pleistocene environment of midwestern United States about 11,000 years ago when the Wisconsinan ice sheet had begun to wane. At Kimmswick, Clovis people exploited a totally different group of animals than that available in the western United States. This included the mastodon. The Kimmswick Site is one of the more important in North America, and it has been incorporated into a Missouri state park, Mastodon State Park, easily reached from Interstate 55 south of St. Louis.

Contemporary with the mastodons in the spruce-forest zone lived the moose and the stag-moose. The latter is now extinct but was a browsing musk-ox-like animal adapted to forest and woodland (Fig. 9-20). Extinct, too, is the giant beaver (*Castoroides ohioensis*) that weighed up to 500 pounds and measured as much as four feet in body length (Fig. 9-21) and the graceful, slender-legged fugitive deer (*Sangamona fugitiva*) (Fig. 9-22). The fugitive deer was first described from fossils discovered in Tennessee and named after the Sangamonian Interglacial Stage and Sangamon County, Illinois. During this interglacial stage, about 125,000 years ago, the giant tortoise *Geochelone crassiscutata* lived here. Its shell was about four feet long, and when living *Geochelone* probably weighed about 100 pounds. Several fragments of a juvenile have been collected by Illinois State Museum scientists near Fillmore, in eastern Montgomery County. Its presence indicates that the Sangamonian climate in Illinois was dry and warm, with temperatures in winter never falling below freezing.

In the open and grassy woodlands, or savanna, farther beyond the ice sheet and in the western plains of the continent ranged horses, camels, bison, large cats (both biting and stabbing forms), bears, wolves, elk, antelopes, at least two kinds of mammoths without arctic adaptation, as well as mastodons. Bison roamed the plains in herds as large as those seen by Europeans when they reached North America. At least seven kinds of bison lived at different times during the Pleistocene, and one of the earlier of these, *Bison latifrons*, was a colossal creature with a horn-spread of six feet (Fig. 9-23). Arriving from South America were the ancestors of the

Fig. 9-20. The stag-moose was a large, mooselike animal with huge, palm-shaped antlers. (Painting by R. Bruce Horsfall, courtesy of American Philosophical Society)

Fig. 9-21. The giant beaver was about the size of a modern black bear. It did not have a paddlelike tail as do modern beavers but a rodentlike tail instead. (Reconstruction by W. Stone and J. Saunders, Illinois State Museum)

ground sloth (*Glossotherium harlani*), now also extinct, an apparently clumsy beast with the bulk of an ox, short-legged, and curiously "club" or fold-footed (Fig. 9-24). Throughout the United States the teeming life might have approached in numbers and variety that which can be seen on the vast grass plains in East or South Africa today.

Why did 70 percent of these animals vanish forever immediately before, during, and after the great melt of the Wisconsinan ice sheet? The rich Pleistocene fauna of large animals made Illinois and the rest of continental United States big-game country for about two million years. Surely,

Fig. 9-22. The fugitive deer was a deer about the size of today's white-tailed deer. Unlike the modern white-tailed deer, the so-called "stilt-legged" deer preferred open forest environments. (Reconstruction by W. Stone and J. Saunders, Illinois State Museum)

change in climatic conditions, as is so often suggested, could not be the whole answer. Animals could possibly adapt to both Arctic and more temperate conditions, as evidenced by the mammoth. Was the arrival of human groups into North America sometime between 20,000 and 12,000 years ago part of the reason? Some think so. The sharp-edged quartz and stone projectile points and other innovative weaponry and tools were utilized for the systematic killing and butchering of mammoth herds.

And what caused the Pleistocene Ice Ages in the first place? Will another episode of extensive continent-wide glaciation again affect North America? No one, unfortunately, has these answers although many theories have been offered to explain the Pleistocene glacial episodes. Can you imagine the consequences if glaciers again reached New York City, St. Louis, and Seattle? Imagine Chicago under mile-high ice. Not only would much habitable and productive land be locked up under glacial ice, but sea level would drop hundreds of feet leaving our major coastal cities high and dry, many hundreds of miles inland.

Be that as it may, Illinois no longer is in the frigid grip of glacial ice—at least for the time being—and the great herds are gone forever. But its landforms are here to appreciate and study, and countless numbers of fossils remain to be unearthed, studied, and preserved. And the materials carried here from elsewhere as a consequence of the several ice advances and retreats have provided Illinois the basis for some of the richest and most productive soil to be found anywhere in the world.

Fig. 9-23. The giant bison was an enormous creature with a high hump and spreading, slightly curved horns. Now extinct, the giant bison was the largest bison to live in North America. (Reconstruction by W. Stone and J. Saunders, Illinois State Museum)

No discussion of the Pleistocene Ice Ages would be complete without reference to the Great Lakes, and because Lake Michigan cannot be considered separately, all five will be mentioned. All are inextricably interconnected. The Great Lakes are among the most expansive and deepest bodies of fresh water in the world (Fig. 9-25). One-fifth of all the fresh water on Earth occurs here, a surface area that covers 94,710 square miles. These five adjoining lakes—Superior, Michigan, Huron, Erie, and Ontario—act as a drainage for their tributary rivers, of which there are hundreds throughout the Great Lakes Basin. Each lake's water moves through its watershed to the Atlantic Ocean by way of the St. Lawrence River. The Great Lakes system moves nearly 6.5 billion gallons of water into the St. Lawrence River every hour. Despite this awesome flow, it would take about 200 years for a drop of water along the western shore of Lake Superior, say at the city of Duluth, Minnesota, to pass through the lake and enter Lake Huron. Another 50 to 75 years would be required for the same drop of water to find its way through Lakes Erie and Ontario into the St. Lawrence River. If perchance it had found its way into Lake Michigan and traveled down to Chicago and back again to the Straits of Mackinac and into Lake Huron, that detour would add another 100 years to the journey.

These five Great Lakes and Minnesota's "10,000 lakes," are at the southern end of an incredibly vast lake region that covers more than half of Canada and includes additional "great lakes" such as Lake Winnipeg, Lake Athabasca, Great Slave Lake, and Great Bear Lake (Fig. 9-26). All are centered in the part of the continent that had undergone extensive and pro-

Fig. 9-24. The Harlan's ground sloth was a lumbering, ox-sized animal capable of rearing up on its stout hind legs to feed on leaves and twigs. Exclusively a plant eater, the ground sloth was equipped with elongated front claws that apparently were used to snag branches and may have been used as defensive weapons. (Reconstruction by W. Stone and J. Saunders, Illinois State Museum)

found modification through Pleistocene glaciation, and all are of glacial origin. The basins occupied by the Great Lakes are to some degree glacially deepened preglacial lowlands. Other lakes are basins in or between moraines, resulting from irregular deposition of glacial material. Still others are kettle lakes in pitted outwash plains or within the glacial ground moraine deposits.

For many years, differences of opinion were expressed as to the extent to which the Great Lake basins were deepened by glacial erosion. All agree, however, that during preglacial time the region was an interconnected lowland that lay above sea level and drained eastward to the Gulf of St. Lawrence. Yet, the bedrock foundation of all the basins, except that of Lake Erie, extends far below sea level—Lake Superior's bedrock floor is 731 feet below sea level; Lake Michigan's is 343 feet below sea level; Lake Ontario's is 532 feet below sea level; and Lake Huron's is 170 feet below sea level. Lake Superior, the largest freshwater body in the world, is 602 feet above sea level and 1,333 feet deep at its maximum. Lake Michigan is not far behind with a depth at maximum of 923 feet. It is a subject of some dispute whether glacical erosion is largely responsible for these great depths or if they have been brought about by land subsidence due to the over-powering weight of the glacial ice. What is known is that the water levels of the lakes stabilized to their present condition about 2,500 years ago.

The history of the Great Lakes has been unraveled mainly by tracing topographic and geologic features that indicate the positions of former shorelines and lake outlets. Reconstructing the lake sequence has provided one of the most challenging and interesting problems in glacial geology.

Fig. 9-25. Lake Michigan and hummocks of wind-blown sand dunes, as seen at Illinois Beach State Park near Zion, Lake County. (Photograph courtesy of Illinois State Geological Survey)

Wave-cut cliffs and related features; beaches and associated off-shore sand and gravel bars; lines of sand dunes behind former shorelines; exposed lake-bottom clays and silts; wide spillways or outlets cut across bedrock or glacial drift, now unused or reoccupied today by undersized streams, streams much too small for the size of the spillway or outlet—all have been used in working out the many phases of Great Lakes history.

The Great Lakes were formed as the Pleistocene glaciers retreated from the region (Fig. 9-27). Several of the lakes, for example, have rounded ends reflecting the rounded contours of the glacial lobes. Lake Michigan is bordered by the Wheaton Morainal Country and provides a good example of lobe-shaped end moraines paralleling a lobe-shaped south shoreline.

The basins now occupied by the Great Lakes are underlain by easily eroded shales and limestones, and in preglacial time this lowland drained eastward to the Gulf of St. Lawrence. How much these lowlands were deepened by glacial scour is unclear; it is difficult to account for the great depths of Lakes Superior and Michigan by either depression under the ice load or through glacial scouring. But it seems that locally, at least, glacial scouring was intense and providing perhaps the essential conditions for the development, in late Wisconsinan time, of a complex series of ice-margin lakes. Names have been given to the original ice-margin lakes that marked the initial phases of lake evolution in each of the lake basins. Lake Maumee was the forerunner of present Lake Erie; Lake Chicago of Lake Michigan; Lake Saginaw of Lake Huron; Lake Duluth of Lake Superior; and Lake Iroquois of Lake Ontario. The complex history of lake evolution, in its simplest analysis, involves a series of changing shore outlines and lake outlets influenced by five factors: an oscillating ice front; irregularities of the topography uncovered by the retreat and advance of the ice front; lowering of lake outlets by erosion; and differential uplift of the land adjacent to the ice front during and following glacial withdrawal.

As a result of the many elevation changes in the lake shorelines, altitude above sea level, and depth, the waters flowed through various outlets at one time or another. These included the Fort Wayne outlet of Lake Maumee to the Wabash Valley; the Chicago outlet via the Des Plaines River to the Illinois River; the St. Croix outlet of Lake Duluth to the Mississippi River; the Imlay, Ubly, and Grand river outlets across Michigan; the Kirkfield and Ottawa river outlets across Ontario; the Syracuse and Rome outlets to the Mohawk and Hudson rivers; and the Susquehanna outlet to Chesapeake Bay. The most continuously used outlet was the Chicago outlet. Except for two low-water phases of Lake Chicago, this outlet was in use all the time. The dried parts of the former, much-larger lakes form some of the best agricultural land, such as the former lake beds of Lake Maumee at the west of Lake Erie and of glacial Lake Saginaw at the head of Saginaw Bay in Michigan.

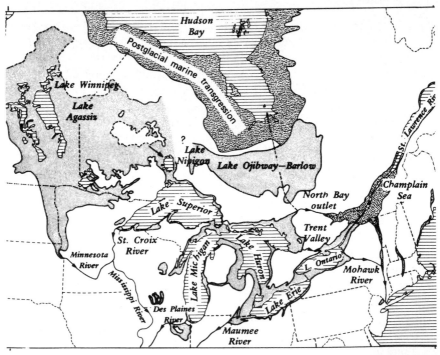

Fig. 9-26. Major glacial lakes of the Great Lakes region showing the principal spillways through which the lakes drained. Areas flooded by the predecessors of the lakes are shaded. (C. W. Stearn, R. L. Carroll, and T. H. Clark, *Geological Evolution of North America,* Third Edition, John Wiley & Sons, 1979, p. 511, reprinted by permission)

Land movements, and the accompanying adjustments in lake elevations and sizes, were caused by regional readjustments to the unloading of
the ice sheets. Today, these adjustments are noticeable in the tilt of the
shoreline features of the ancestral Great Lakes. Such movements are, in
fact, still going on; the northern shores of Lake Superior and Lake Ontario
are tilting southward six to twelve inches each century as the northern lands
rise after being relieved of the weight of the Wisconsinan glacier.

Shipping in the Great Lakes is a vital part of the nation's economy,
despite the fact that these ports are closed much of the winter. In 1959,
channels were deepened and the St. Lawrence Seaway became passable by
all but the largest ocean-going vessels. About 80 percent of the world's ships
can now proceed as far as Duluth—more than 2,300 miles inland.

The Great Lakes are important, too, for hydroelectric power and for
fisheries. They provide about two percent of the country's fish production,
mostly lake herring, whitefish, lake trout, perch, pike, and suckers.
Chicago withdraws more than 1.25 million gallons of water a minute for
domestic use and to flush its treated sewage down the Illinois River. When
the Great Lakes reached their current sizes and shapes, another fascinating
chapter—one of particular importance in terms of shaping the Illinois landscape—the Pleistocene, drew to a close.

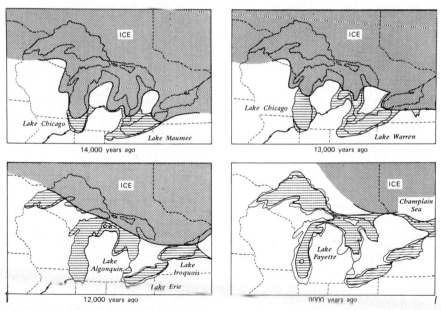

Fig. 9-27. This series of maps shows how the Great Lakes changed as the glacial sheet
continued to retreat. (J. J. Fagan, *View of the Earth: An Introduction to Geology*,
Holt, Rinehart and Winston, Inc., 1965, p. 326, reprinted by permission of CBS College Publishing)

Chapter 10
Epilogue

With the withdrawal of the Wisconsinan glacier, Illinois's modern landscape emerged. It had long been in the making, and the geologic legacy is there for all to read. Farmland has replaced almost all of the former prairies, and the woodlands have been drastically reduced in size. Erosion and deposition of sand along the Lake Michigan shorefront alter its appearance with each passing storm. But overall, in the slow pace of geologic time, little more will change in our lifetime. An occasional minor earthquake might be felt, locally twisting and changing the configuration of the ground. The valleys will become imperceptibly deeper, and many will become wider as the rivers and streams meander slowly toward the sea, taking with them the valuable soil, our inheritance from the Pleistocene Ice Ages on which so much of our economy is based. Wind will pick up sediment from here and deposit it there, only to take it again and leave it somewhere else.

And as I ponder the many ways our lands have been shaped and reshaped by the relentless forces of nature over the past 1.5 billion years, I am reminded of a catastrophic and cataclysmic event that struck the region about 175 years ago. That event radically changed the face of the land within a relatively small area. Had it occurred today, or should it happen again tomorrow, or within the next years, the tragic consequences could not begin to be measured.

Early in the nineteenth century, three powerful earthquakes rocked the five-corners region where Illinois, Missouri, Arkansas, Kentucky, and Tennessee are close together. Why the quakes occurred is still only partly understood. More important perhaps is the question of whether other earthquakes could occur in the future. To this question the answer is "yes."

Facing page. The Pine Hills are composed of early Devonian, thin-bedded, chert-bearing limestone and face the Big Muddy tributary of the Mississippi River near Grand Tower, Jackson County. These 350-foot-high bluffs have been exposed by erosion rather than uplift along a fault.

The dreaded earthquake is one of nature's most persistently frequent cataclysms—and the most destructive to lives and property. "It is a bitter and humiliating thing," remarked Charles Darwin in 1835 upon witnessing the effects of a great earthquake in Chile, "to see works, which have cost man so much time and labor, overthrown in one minute." Down through the centuries, it has been our common but "hard-to-believe-that-it-happened" experience to find, as did Darwin, that "the earth, the very emblem of solidity, has moved beneath our feet like a thin crust over a fluid."

More than a million tremors occur each year, every 30 seconds, day in and day out. About 800,000 of these are scarcely strong enough to rattle a teacup in its saucer, and without the sensitive modern instrument called the seismograph, they would pass unnoticed. Hundreds more produce significant alterations in the face of the land. But only about 20 each year cause the most severe distortions; when they strike heavily populated areas they take a tragic toll.

Such were the distortions of the land that occurred in the region of New Madrid, Missouri, on 16 December 1811, and 23 January and 7 February 1812. The seismograph had not been invented yet; the principal witnesses were the less than 3,000 persons, mostly frontier trappers and their families, living in this Mississipi River area (Fig. 10-1). John Bradbury, a noted Scottish botanist, was on a Mississippi flatboat just below New Madrid enroute to New Orleans at the time of the shock and provided one of the most vivid descriptions of the the quakes. Charles Lyell, the great English geologist, visited the site in March 1846 and commented on the effects of the disturbances. In the immediate damage area, large tracts of forests crashed to the ground and giant fissures opened up, some so broad that no horse could jump them. At New Madrid, terrified residents leaped from their beds—the earthquakes all occurred in the early morning, at 2:00 a.m., 9:00 a.m., and 3:45 a.m., respectively—and saw their cabins splintering around them. Eerie flashes of light like distant lightning streaked the sky, and the air was heavy with sulfurous fumes. Geysers of white quartz sand and black coal grit spouted from the ground, dotting the landscape of the bottomlands for miles. Hundreds of miles from New Madrid, the early morning shocks were so powerful that windows rattled and chandeliers shook in Washington, D.C.; pendulum clocks were stopped in Charleston, South Carolina; church bells were set tolling in Richmond, Virginia; and residents in Pittsburgh, Pennsylvania, were awakened. Nearer, in Kentucky, naturalist John James Audubon remarked that "the ground rose and fell in successive furrows like the ruffled waters of a lake. The earth waved like a field of corn before a breeze."

By the time the Earth stopped shaking, a total of 1,874 shocks had occurred between 16 December and 15 March, eight of which were classified as violent, 10 as very severe, and 35 as moderate but alarming. The land-

Fig. 10-1. The New Madrid region in eastern Missouri was rocked by three powerful earthquakes in the winter of 1811-1812. During the earthquake the Mississippi turned into a raging river as depicted in this 19th-century lithograph. Should an earthquake of such magnitude occur again, the consequences would be devastating. (Illustration courtesy of State Historical Society of Missouri, Columbia)

scape changed beyond recognition. Fields and riverbanks were crisscrossed by a maze of furrows and deep fractures, and thousands of acres of prairie were converted into swamp. On the Mississippi, a lake bed was raised to become dry land, several lakes were created where none had been before. Reelfoot Lake in Tennessee was enlarged and deepened and Lake St. Francis, 40 miles long and one-half mile wide, was formed on the Arkansas-Missouri border. Islands disappeared, and in places the Mississippi's banks collapsed, temporarily damming the river. A vertical fault displacement of its bed caused the river to run backward for a time. New Madrid was leveled and the land under it slumped 15 feet. Despite all this disruption, casualities were few—a man was buried under his roof in New Madrid, and some people drowned when their boats capsized in the raging Mississippi.

Efforts to explain these quakes—which all subsequent seismological studies indicated should not have occurred with such fury, if even at all—continue today and with increasing urgency. The last significant quake in the area was on 31 October 1895 (Fig. 10-2). This earthquake struck shortly after 5:00 a.m., awakening people throughout the region as their

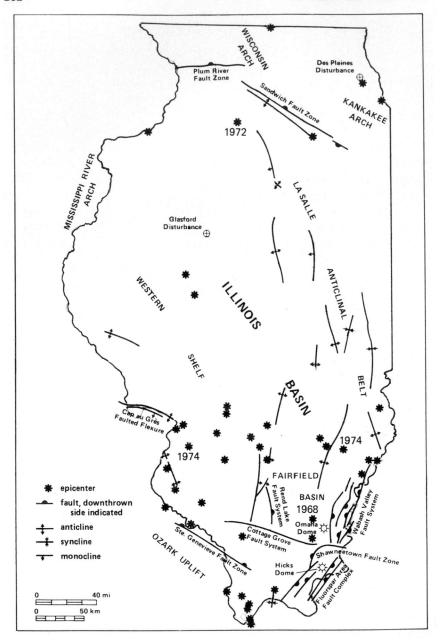

Fig. 10-2. Map of Illinois showing structures such as basins and domes, anticlines and synclines, arches, and fault zones. Centers of historical earthquakes with intensities of V or greater on the Modified Mercalli Intensity Scale are shown. Intensity V is classified "rather strong" (felt generally; most sleepers awakened). There is no evidence that any faults seen at the surface have moved in the past thousand years. (Map courtesy of Illinois State Geological Survey)

beds shook and moved. In Springfield, some residents thought their houses were being invaded by burglers; others fled fearing their furnaces were about to explode. Fourteen years later, in 1909, a series of minor earthquakes shook the Midwest, with one on July 18 bringing down chimneys, breaking windows, and cracking plaster in Petersburg, in Menard County northwest of Springfield. This particular quake remains something of a mystery because its center, north of Petersburg, is in an area not known to have any faults or other subsurface structural weaknesses.

Tremors are regularly recorded in the Memphis and St. Louis areas, but most can be detected only with the aid of instruments. With each passing year the conditions for another earthquake improve and the probability of a repeat event increases. Recent research has shown that major quakes occur in this region on an average of every 600 years; there is a seven percent chance that a major quake will occur in any fifty-year period. These figures would be comforting if earthquakes obeyed the law of averages, but they do not. For what had been wilderness in 1811 has become the populous heartland of America. An earthquake of similar intensity today would endanger at least 12 million people from Little Rock, Arkansas, and Memphis, Tennessee, to Evansville, Indiana, and Cincinnati, Ohio; and from St. Louis, Missouri, to Peoria, Illinois. Cities as distant as Chicago, and Dallas, Texas, could be affected (Fig. 10-3). Property damage could run in excess of $50 billion; the three New Madrid earthquakes of 1811-1812 were the most severe to have jolted the continental United States, far surpassing the famous San Francisco earthquake of 1906.

Earthquakes occur when crustal rock thousands of feet below the surface, for some reason stressed beyond their limits of strength, suddenly snap and release this pent-up energy much like a rubber band stressed beyond its limit of strength. Foreshocks frequently precede the main shock, and aftershocks, as happened in 1811-1812, usually occur for months thereafter. Earthquakes are associated with faults, natural fractures in the Earth's rocky crust, along which the crust is now moving or has moved in the past. The best known is the San Andreas Fault in northern California and it is of paramount concern to San Franciscans because of its known historic activity. Strangely—or so it seemed until the late 1970s—no faults in the New Madrid region capable of resulting in such powerful earthquakes were known to exist.

Seismographs, sufficiently sophisticated to record and measure an earthquake, were not developed until late in the nineteenth century. Delicately balanced objects, bowls brimful with water, and other simple but clever ways were used to monitor Earth movements. No reliable method was available to obtain the necessary data that would provide an understanding of earthquake dynamics until the invention of the seismograph. Then, in 1935, Carl Richter at the Seismological Laboratory of the California Institute of Technology devised a scale that accurately

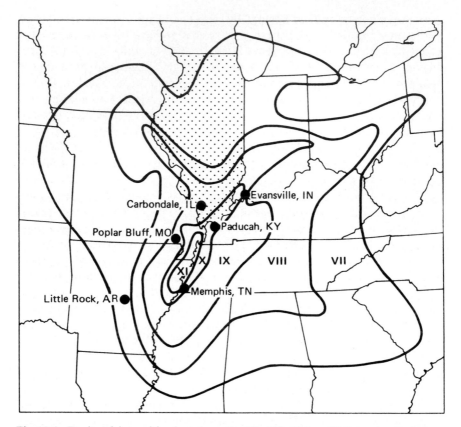

Fig 10-3. Regional intensities based on the Modified Mercalli Intensity Scale suggesting the possible effects of an earthquake as severe as those of 1811-1812 quakes if the center of the quake again occurred in the New Madrid area. On this scale, an intensity of XI is "very disastrous" (few buildings remain standing; bridges destroyed; all services [railway, pipes, and cables] are disrupted; great landslides and floods can occur), and VII is "very strong" (general alarm; walls crack; plaster falls). (Source of information, United States Geological Survey)

measures the energy released by an earthquake. This Richter Scale, as it is known, measures the magnitude of an earthquake, that is, the amount of energy released at the time of a quake. It is a logarithmic scale in that an increase of one-tenth of a unit indicates a tenfold increase in the amount of released energy. On this now commonly used reference scale, property damage in nearby communities begins at magnitude 5 and increases logarithmically to nearly total destruction for earthquakes with a magnitude in excess of 8, which occurs somewhere in the world about once every 5 to 10 years. The New Madrid earthquakes would have registered magnitudes of 8.6, 8.4, and 8.7, respectively, on the Richter Scale. No earthquakes larger than 8.9 have ever been recorded, a limitation not on the measuring scale but of the Earth itself. The disastrous earthquake at Anchorage, Alaska, on 27 March 1964, recorded a magnitude of 8.6, or three million times as great as that of an earthquake of magnitude 5. For comparison, the first atomic bomb tested in the New Mexico desert in July 1945 released energy equivalent to a magnitude of 5.

Almost all earthquakes occur along narrow bands that circle the Pacific Ocean, the mid-ocean regions, and the mountains and high plateau systems of southern Europe, Turkey, northern Iran, and the China-India border regions. Indeed, about 98 percent of the world's earthquakes take place in these regions, and the concept of plate tectonics quite nicely explains the reasons for this global seismic activity. In Chapter 2 it was pointed out that the Earth's 10-mile-thick crust is divided into about eight large plates, and each is in constant slow movement relative to the other. Where these plates meet is where most, if not almost all, earthquakes occur. The Pacific Plate meets the North American Plate, for example, along the San Andreas Fault; the inexorable movement of several inches per century is accompanied by earthquakes in San Francisco and northern California. Where the Nazca Plate meets the South American Plate along the Andes Mountains, the inexorable crustal movements cause powerful quakes in countries such as Chile. But why earthquakes are felt within a plate, far from its active and mobile boundary, and with the power that occurred at New Madrid, remains largely a mystery although much has been learned about the geology of New Madrid. Seismologists feel confident that another major quake, magnitude 7.5 or greater, is likely to occur. But when is difficult to say even in those regions where they are known to occur with some regularity as in southern California. Earthquakes do not follow the laws of averages, so predictions of an impending earthquake is almost impossible. Even so, the Federal Emergency Management Agency in 1984 granted $300,000 to the Central United States Earthquake Consortium to use in compiling an emergency plan for Illinois, Missouri, Arkansas, Indiana, Kentucky, and Tennessee.

Important clues have recently been uncovered that suggest a solution to the mystery. Teams of government and university scientists have used new techniques, including some that have been employed in oil prospecting for more than a decade, to compile a convincing array of revealing data. It appears that a long and deep break, referred to as a rift, exists in the North American Plate; it formed at least 500 million years ago, perhaps even earlier in Precambrian time. A rift is usually bounded on both its long sides by faults and is caused by a major subsidence of the crust. This particular rift, known as the Reelfoot Rift, extends all the way through the crust to a depth of at least 25 miles and is more than 200 miles long and about 50 miles wide. Why it is here, within the plate rather than along a plate boundary where fractures usually occur, is not known. Everywhere it lies buried beneath a thick wedge of comparatively soft sediments deposited in what had been a slowly sinking embayment of the Gulf of Mexico within the past 70 million years (Fig. 10-4). New Madrid, then, about 70 million years ago would have been a coastal city as today are New Orleans, Louisiana, and Biloxi, Mississippi. Because these embayment rocks are soft, the geologic record of long-term fault movements associated with this mid-continent rift is not well preserved. In effect, the sediments of the embayment veil the deep earthquake-related features and necessitate the use of expensive, sophisticated geophysical methods that can "see" through the sediments and into the rift-bearing basement rock. And this evidence did not materialize until the late 1970s.

A complex network of faults exists in southern Illinois north of the Mississippi Embayment (Fig. 10-4). Both Hicks Dome and the fluorite mining district, for example, are located within this fault system. While many minor earthquakes do occur in southern Illinois, there is no hard evidence that any of these faults have been displaced since Pleistocene time. Although the faults in southern Illinois appear to be extensions of the buried Reelfoot Rift—extensions of the New Madrid Seismic Zone as it also is called—geologists tend not to link together the two earthquake areas. The fault zones in southern Illinois are neither actively developing nor are they slipping in response to earthquakes that originate elsewhere.

The net result of the new geologic data suggests that the Earth's crust beneath the embayment sediments, within the Reelfoot Rift, is badly weakened. As the North American Plate continues in its westward drift and slides against the Pacific Plate at the San Andreas Fault, its bottom drags against the still deeper, underlying mantle. Stress on the weakened zone centered at New Madrid, caused by the friction between the crustal plate and the underlying mantle, is released periodically in the deeply buried rift zone. And the surface shakes.

Man clings to the skin of a planet involved in the elemental forces of creation—ever-changing, never at rest. Earthquakes are an integral part of this change, no different than the processes of erosion, of volcanism, of the deposition of sediment in a lake, stream, or ocean (Fig. 10-5). There is nothing mystical or exceptional about them. An understanding of plate tectonics, sea-floor spreading, and the relative motions of Earth's plates places the earthquake in a different perspective and raises fresh hopes of predicting, surviving, and possibly one day controlling its outbursts. Earthquake prediction is at the cutting edge of basic geologic science, and substantial research programs are underway principally in China, Japan, and the Soviet Union. In the United States, about $17 million is being spent each year on prediction and another $43 million on a research program including earthquake-hazard assessment, the engineering of buildings to resist earthquakes, and studies of the fundamental nature of earthquakes. Progress on short-term prediction has been slower than workers had hoped a decade ago when early successes were reported by both Soviet and American re-

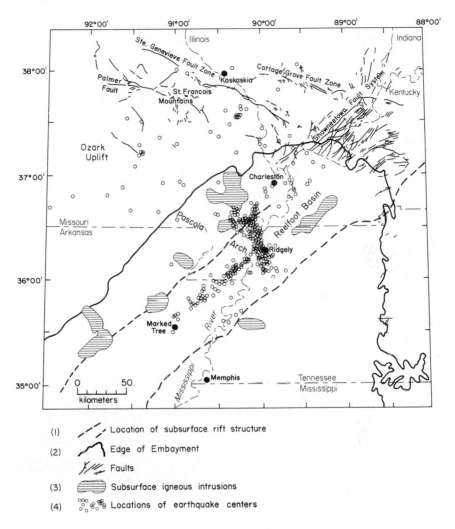

Fig. 10-4. Simplified map of the faults in the New Madrid region showing **(1)** the northeast-southwest-trending rift structure; **(2)** the edge of the Mississippi Embayment; **(3)** igneous intrusions of peridotite and similar dense iron rich rock bodies; and **(4)** the locations of earthquakes detected from July 1974 to June 1977. Note the numerous faults, none known to be active, that extend beyond the cover of softer Coastal Plain sediments into the harder bedrock of southern Illinois.

searchers. On the other hand, progress in long-term prediction and in the understanding of how earthquakes occur has been substantial.

Will Earth scientists be assertive when they are faced with the responsibility to forecast an impending earthquake? They may well be reluctant to issue a warning; the costs of a false one are potentially great. And will citizens respond to such a warning? There was reluctance to respond to forecast warnings issued prior to the devastating Mount St. Helens eruptions when some of the signs were clearly more visible than any for an earthquake. Nevertheless, the potential consequence of a next great earthquake argues strongly that all reasonable efforts be made to predict the event in the deep rift zone of the mid-continent—and that all efforts be made to respond to such a prediction. For today and the future, people must learn to live with that inescapable certainty expressed best by historian Will Durant that "civilization exists by geological consent, subject to change without notice." Such are the birth pangs of down-to-earth geology; Illinois is not exempt.

Fig. 10-5. Grand Tower Limestone exposed in a small bluff facing the Mississippi River at the "Bake Oven" north of Grand Tower, Jackson County. Originally horizontal, these middle Devonian limestone strata tipped steeply to the east (to the right) when the crust was uplifted and torn along fault zones by past earthquake activity. See Figures 10-2 and 10-4 for the distribution of some of these faults.

Appendix 1
Counties and County Seats of Illinois

ILLINOIS

⭐ State capital and county seat
• County seats
▪▪▪ Canal

0   25   50 mi.

0   25   50   75 km.

Appendix 2
Sources of Geologic Information

Textbooks and other references that discuss the general principles and concepts of geology are available in public libraries under two major categories: physical geology and historical geology. Several titles are credited in illustration captions in this book.

In addition, a popular series of booklets called the *Golden Guides* are especially straightforward and inexpensive. In this series are three titles, *Geology; Fossils;* and *Rocks and Minerals.* They provide an excellent introduction and can be obtained from the publisher.

Western Publishing Company, Inc.
Department M
1220 Mound Avenue
Racine, WI 53404

The Illinois State Museum provides free of charge a "List of Publications" that describes the geologic publications it currently has available. Also, a free subscription to *The Living Museum,* an illustrated quarterly magazine featuring articles about the geology of Illinois as well as its archaeology, art, and natural history, is available by writing to the Editor, *The Living Museum,* Illinois State Museum, Spring and Edwards Streets, Springfield, IL 62706.

The Illinois State Museum offers field trips in geology, natural history, and archaeology throughout Illinois and the Midwest by charter coach. A modest charge covers costs. For further information, contact the Illinois State Museum's Education Section at (217) 782-5993.

The Illinois State Geological Survey provides a free copy of their "List of Publications" that describes all publications in the geological sciences they currently have available. The Geological Survey also has a free brochure entitled "Educational Resources," available to teachers only. It describes the literature and educational materials currently available for school use in the geological sciences. Field trips throughout Illinois are offered by the Illinois State Geological Survey's Educational Extension Public Relations Unit. Usually two trips in the autumn and two trips in the spring are offered. Each of the four trips are held in different areas of the state. These are free and conducted by car caravan. A detailed guidebook is provided free on the day of the field trip and is for sale thereafter. In addition, the Illinois State Geological Survey is an official distribution agency for Illinois topographic maps produced by the United States Geological Survey. Further information can be obtained from the following address.

Illinois State Geological Survey
Educational Extension Public Relations Unit
Natural Resources Building
615 East Peabody Drive
Champaign, IL 61820
Telephone: (217) 344-1481

Listed below are the addresses of the geological surveys for states adjacent to Illinois. These agencies can provide information similar to that described for Illinois, including publication lists.

Missouri Department of Natural Resources
Division of Geology and Land Survey
P. O. Box 250
Rolla, MO 65401
Telephone: (314) 364-1752

Geological and Natural History Survey
University of Wisconsin — Extension
1815 University Avenue
Madison, WI 53705
Telephone: (608) 262-1705

Iowa Geological Survey
123 North Capitol Street
Iowa City, IA 52242
Telephone: (319) 338-1173

Kentucky Geological Survey
University of Kentucky
311 Breckinridge Hall
Lexington, KY 40506
Telephone: (606) 257-5863

Indiana Geological Survey
Indiana University
611 North Walnut Grove
Bloomington, IN 47405
Telephone: (812) 335-2862

People interested in rocks, minerals, fossils, and geology often join a local mineral and rock club that meets on a regular basis. To find out if such a club is near you, your library may have on file the April issue of a monthly publication, *The Lapidary Journal.* Its April issue, titled the "Rockhound Buyers Guide," lists the names and addresses of clubs throughout the United States. Listed also are all the businesses in the United States that deal in rocks and minerals, lapidary supplies, or other geology-related items.

The Lapidary Journal
P. O. Box 80937
San Diego, CA 92138

Glossary

This glossary is not intended to be exhaustive. Instead, it provides a handy reference for some major concepts and terms.

Anticline. A fold in rock, with the core or center containing older rocks.

Basin. A circular or elliptical depression in bedrock with the rock sloping gently down toward the center from all directions.

Bedrock. A general term for the rock that underlies soil or other unconsolidated surface material.

Clastic. Rock or sediment composed mainly of broken fragments derived from pre-existing rocks or minerals that were transported from their places of origin. Also called fragmental rock.

Composition. The type of minerals, mineral and rock fragments, and fossils that are present in a rock.

Crust. The approximately 10-mile-thick outermost layer of the Earth.

Cyclothem. A series of strata deposited by a single sedimentary cycle. Typically, cyclothems are associated with an unstable interior basin that alternated between marine transgressions and regressions during the Pennsylvanian Period.

Dome. A circular or elliptical anticlinal uplift with the rock layers sloping gently away in all directions.

Downbuckle. A downward bending of rock that produces synclines and basins.

Drift. Rock material transported by a glacier and deposited directly from the ice or by running water emanating from the glacier.

Element. The basic, submicroscopic unit of matter that contains a definite number of atomic particles, such as electrons, protons, and neutrons.

Epeirogeny. Vertical movements that have affected large parts of the continent.

Escarpment. A long, more or less continuous, cliff that is produced by erosion or faulting and that breaks the continuity of the land by separating two levels or gently sloping surfaces.

Extrusion. The emitting of lava and other eruptive material onto the Earth's surface. This material then forms igneous rock.

Fault. A zone where rock was fractured and subsequently displaced.

Fold. A bend in rock strata produced by stresses within the crust.

Foliation. Thin, leaflike layers of minerals in certain metamorphic rocks such as schist or gneiss.

Formation. The basic rock unit in the local classification of rocks. It consists of a body of rock characterized by a general uniformity of composition, texture, origin, and fossils.

Fossil. Remaining trace or imprint of a plant or animal that has been preserved by natural processes in the Earth's crust since some past geologic time.

Fragmental. See clastic.

Hydrothermal. A thin and watery magma in the final stages of igneous activity when it consists mainly of hot water and dissolved gases. The hydrothermal solution is strongly enriched in light-weight and volatile elements such as fluorine but may contain heavier elements such as lead and gold.

Igneous rock. Rock derived from the solidification of magma beneath the Earth's surface and lava on the Earth's surface.

Intrusion. The emplacement of magma into pre-existing rock. The result may be a sill, dike, or other body of igneous rock.

Kettle. A bowl-shaped depression without surface drainage in a glaciated region. It often contains a lake, swamp, or bog, and possibly their sediment record. A kettle forms by the melting of a large, detached block of stagnant glacier ice wholly or partly buried by drift.

Lava. Molten silicate material originating within the Earth. This extrusive material crystallizes into igneous rock.

Loess. A widespread, homogeneous, usually unstratified, unconsolidated but coherent, buff to light yellow or yellow-brown, highly calcareous, fine-grained blanket of wind-blown dust originating during the Pleistocene Ice Ages. When exposed, loess stands in steep or nearly vertical faces.

Magma. Molten silicate material originating within the Earth. This intrusive material crystallizes into igneous rock.

Mantle. The 2,000-mile-thick zone beneath the crust of the Earth.

Marine. Pertaining to the sea or ocean.

Metamorphic rock. Rock produced by mineralogical and chemical changes in pre-existing rock in response to changes in temperature, pressure, stress, and chemical environment deep in the Earth's crust.

Mineral. A naturally formed chemical element or compound with a geometric arrangement of its atomic structure that may form a crystal.

Moraine. A mound, ridge, or other distinct accumulation of unsorted, unstratified till deposited mainly by direct action of glacier ice. The shape of a moraine is not controlled by the surface on which it lies.

Orogeny. The process of mountain formation.

Physiographic province. A region with all parts similar in geologic structure and rock types and that consequently had a comparatively similar geologic history and landscape evolution.

Plate tectonics. Global activity based on a model of large, broad, thick plates that move relative to each other on the Earth's surface and that are carried by powerful currents in the upper mantle. Continents form a part of the plates.

Regression. The retreat of the sea from land areas and the evidence of such withdrawal.

Rift. A deep, elongate, depressed crustal block bounded by faults on its long sides.

Rock. A naturally formed, consolidated material composed of one or more minerals and showing some degree of mineralogic and textural consistency.

Rock-forming mineral. Any one of about a dozen minerals that occurs commonly in rocks. Included is quartz, feldspar, and calcite.

Sedimentary rock. Rock derived from fragmental material. The fragments originated from surface weathering of pre-existing rocks and were transported, accumulated, and consolidated by natural processes.

Slopewash. Soil and loose rock transported down a slope by broad sheets of running water that are not confined to distinct channels.

Stratification. The accumulation or deposition of materials in layers.

Striae (striations). Superficial scratches, tiny furrows, or threadlike lines, usually parallel to each other, inscribed on a rock surface through the action of a glacier.

Stratum. A distinct layer of homogeneous sedimentary materials of any thickness, visibly separable from other layers above and below. Plural: strata.

Structure. The general attitude, arrangement, or relative positions of the rock masses of a region or area. Structures are produced by uplift and displacement of the rock and include folds and faults.

Syncline. A fold in rock with the core or center containing younger rocks.

Tectonics. Pertaining to the forces involved in producing geologic structures. Included is a study of the mutual relations, origin, and evolution of these forces and structures.

Terrestrial. Pertaining to nonmarine or land areas.

Texture. The physical appearance of a rock and the relationship among the component minerals or sediment particles, including their size and shape.

Till. Unsorted and unstratified drift, usually unconsolidated, deposited directly by and underneath a glacier and consisting of a mixture of clay, sand, gravel, and boulders varying widely in size and shape.

Transgression. The spread of the sea over land areas and the evidence of such advance.

Unconformity. An interruption in the geologic record where a rock unit is overlain by another that is not next in the succession but is considerably younger. Implied in this relationship is uplift and erosion with loss of the intervening record.

Uniformitarianism. The fundamental principle that geologic processes and natural laws now operating to modify the Earth's crust have acted in the same manner and with the same intensity throughout geologic time.

Uparch. An uplift of rock that produces anticlines and domes.

INDEX

Page numbers in boldface refer to illustrations.